HOW TO MAKE MONEY IN YOUR PJS

How I inadvertently built and grew a home-based passive income and how you can do it deliberately

BY BON DOBBS

First Edition

ISBN: 978-1-329-34323-8

ISBN 978-1-329-34323-8

Table of Contents

PREFACE

My regular readers, those that have read my books and joined my community, may be taken aback by this book. They may think: "Bon Dobbs is no expert in passive income!" They would be right to think this.

I am no expert in passive income. I instead will relate to you my experience – how I bumbled my way toward developing a passive income. In fact, I wrote this book for the exact same reasons I wrote my other books. I discovered, through trial and error, something that worked. I'd like to share that with you.

I still have a passion for emotional skills and relating to people with emotional regulation issues. I write my other books about this subject and will continue to do so in the future. This book is something of an aside for me. I just noticed that I have been able to inadvertently create a passive income and wanted to share how I did it.

People say that experience is our best asset. I agree. In this book, you will find my experience and hopefully you will be able to learn from my mistakes.

When I first started writing this book, I was not planning on using Bon Dobbs as the author, because I didn't want to sully my brand as an "expert" in emotional skills. However, I soon discovered that it would be much more valuable to my readers to understand my real life experiences, rather than a generic, anonymous version of them. I decided to come clean with my actual experience such that my readers can research me and confirm what I say in this book.

I sincerely hope that my experience will be valuable to you, and you can avoid the mistakes I made in the last ten years. If you do as I say instead of doing as I did, you can build a passive income in much less time than I did.

If you just implement one of the many methods I talk about in this book, you'll surely get a passive income at the level I have built - and probably much more!

INTRODUCTION

First off, let me say: I did everything wrong. Yet, it still worked. You can learn from my mistakes and missteps. You can do it right the first time.

Last Monday morning from midnight to six A.M., while I slept comfortably in my bed, I made $112.83. How much did you make?

This book explains how to develop a passive income online. A "passive income" is an annuity stream from one-time work. This very book is an example of passive income for me. I wrote the book, published it, and I receive a royalty stream from sales of the book. I don't have to do any additional work on the book. I just sit back and collect royalties.

I will explain in these pages how you too can develop a passive income from various sources on the Internet. I will present these sources from the ones that have made me the most money to those that have made the least and tell you why each generates a revenue stream of the given size. I am going to hold the most lucrative for last, but it is one that I am still striving to develop. It is still a dream in my experience at this point, but it has the potential to eclipse all the others combined.

In an effort to provide disclosure, I currently make about $7,500 a year of passive income. I hope that by further implementing the methods that I will disclose in this book, I can increase that amount.

However, the $7,500 is "found money" – I don't have to do too much additional work to generate that cash. Some of these methods do require ongoing efforts, and I will note what that effort is to enable you to follow the path toward a passive income.

I have a day job. Obviously, $7,500 a year is not enough for me to quit my day job, but this figure has been increasing a little bit every month over the last few years. I hope that one day, as I implement each of these methods more fully, that figure will continue to grow.

Yet, I stumbled into $7,500 a year. I had no plan or design. I was just passionate about my subject. I didn't start for the money. As time went on, I learned from my mistakes. I learned how to increase my passive income with little effort.

You can gain from my experience. You can turn my experience into a fully-designed, full-fledged effort that is likely to make more than I do within the first year.

What would an additional $7,500 a year mean to your life? What if you could generate that income while you're asleep or on vacation?

I'm not an Internet sensation in any sense of the word. I quietly make this money, without too much expense. I like to be quiet about it for various reasons. Perhaps you would like to develop a passive income in a quiet way - a way that doesn't require too much attention to you as a person. If so, my experience will be very valuable to you. Suffice it to say that these methods will probably not make you into a millionaire or a famous person. Yet, if you want to get extra cash – found money – these methods are proven to work effectively.

I also make this money without too much day-to-day work. I like it that way as well. I don't want to have more than one full-time job. If I had to do a large amount of work, it wouldn't be a passive income then would it?

I will spend some time on marketing in this book, but I have by no means cracked the art of standing out in the crowded Internet space. Getting noticed just enough to generate income is important, and it is an on-going issue for everyone who uses the Internet to make money.

The point of this book is to explain to you, from my experience, how you can develop a passive income of several hundred dollars a month (and possibly much, much more, depending on your implementation) while doing as little work as possible. If that appeals to you, read on!

Before I close this introduction, let me just note that my passive income is not all about money. It's about passion as well. I passionately pursue the subject I write about.

I enjoy helping people with the materials I produce. I don't even really do it for the money; I do it for the satisfaction of helping other people. The passive income that these materials provide is just an added benefit. The work that I engage in is much more satisfying than my day job.

If you can find a subject or an activity that supplies satisfaction as well as income, good for you! If it's only income that you seek, this book will help you as well. Now, let's get to it…

CHAPTER 1: ROYALTIES

For me, royalties are the most lucrative income source. They are also the most passive of all of the methods explained in this book. The book you're reading is providing me with royalties. Granted, the royalty is quite low on each sale.

In the case of printed material, sold through a retailer (think Amazon), on a book priced at $19.95, the royalty varies depending on the length of the book. If a book is about 200 pages and self-published through a service, the royalty is about $2.50 dollars a copy. That's about 12.5% of the retail price.

On an electronic edition of a book, the royalty is generally higher, although the price is lower. This is because the physical, printed material does not need to be produced or shipped to the individual consumer.

The royalty formulas differ within different electronic distribution methods. I will go into great detail about how you get your work in various Internet retail stores. There are pitfalls and ways to gain success. Sometimes the services of these Internet retailers change. I will explain the services and restrictions that were in place at the time of the writing of this book.

I'll explain the royalty formula that I work with below. But first, let me explain a bit about royalties.

A royalty is a payment made to the owner/creator of a work – be it a song, a patent, a book, a trademark or other "works of art." I put works of art in quotes here because the term "art" has a specific meaning in this sense. It doesn't mean "art" like paintings or sculpture – it means a product produced by the exercise of one's know-how, skill or knowledge. The term itself is derived from a time in which the "crown" bestowed natural resource rights (like mining rights) on a commercial entity with the expectation of a licensing payment back to the crown (i.e. The royal government, hence the term "royalty").

In the modern world, artists (or other skilled workers) receive royalties when someone purchases (or licenses) their work. Royalties are paid for books, inventions, music, and many other products. Royalties can even be paid on the know-how contained within a patent. I personally am the inventor of a patented technology, but I don't receive royalties for that invention because I had to sign over my inventor rights to my employer at the time, since I was essentially working on their time with their materials.

What I do receive royalties on is my publications: books and eBooks.

How to find something to write about

Basically, I'm telling you to write a book. If you have musical talent, write a song. If you have programming talent, write an app.

What should you write about? Well, let me tell you my story and how I found the subjects of my books.

Finding my niche

About ten years ago, one of my daughters was having trouble in school. My wife and I decided to do an educational and psychosocial assessment of our, then, eight year old daughter. The assessment was quite expensive and took months of interviews and neuropsychological testing.

When we received the report, what we found was very puzzling. It seemed that our daughter was inconsistent in the results of her educational testing. She scored extremely high on some measures and extremely low on other, related measures. It was odd. Even the tester/counselor was quite puzzled.

The solution to our daughter's performance on these tests was contained in the second half of the report. It turns out that our daughter was unable to regulate her emotions. When she was calm and focused, she would score well on the tests. When she was anxious and afraid, she would score poorly.

The second half of the assessor's report was all about our daughter's emotional state. It told the story of a girl who was easily triggered into emotional states and who was overwhelmed by these states. Our daughter told the assessor stories in which the main character's friends ran away from her forever. She was expecting doom to come to her. She was dreading the future.

Our daughter was naturally much more sensitive than her sisters. This emotional sensitivity translated into inconsistent test performance in poor learning strategies. Essentially, she had an emotional regulation problem.

11

She was easily triggered into emotionality, mostly negative (fear, anger or sadness), and the intensity of the emotions was such that she was unable to think clearly or learn or be comfortable in social situations.

We were at an impasse as to how to proceed. She was a bright girl, doing very well in school when she was not fraught with powerful emotions. Since I cared for her deeply (and still do), I began doing research into conditions that cause emotional regulation problems. I eventually found borderline personality disorder, which is not diagnosed in children. It fits my daughter pretty thoroughly, although some of the adult behaviors associated with this condition had not yet emerged in her.

I began reading all of the existing books on being a loved one of a person with the disorder. I tried all the strategies from each of these books (and there were only a handful at the time, with one being the most popular), but the strategies were not working consistently with my daughter.

I also joined a couple of Internet communities and began reading the experiences of other parents, partners and friends. I developed a close relationship with a few of the community members. Since we shared a common problem, these members were understanding and helped me tremendously.

After researching treatments for the disorder, I discovered Dialectical Behavior Therapy (DBT), which, at the time, was the gold standard for treating borderline personality disorder. In many ways, DBT is still the gold standard. There was only one problem: no therapist offered DBT to children or pre-teens.

After much research, discussion and advisement from some of the experts in the field, who I had contacted out of desperation, I found a therapist near me who had adapted DBT for children. It was a wonderful discovery. I contacted the office of the therapist and he agreed to accept my daughter as a patient.

Since my daughter was a minor, I was encouraged to participate in her therapy to some degree. I would take my daughter once a week to the therapy. For the first six months of the therapy, my daughter did not want to be there and distrusted the therapist. She was essentially silent for six months. I would go into the therapist's office and the therapist and would talk about my daughter as she sat silently on the couch, her arms crossed and an angry look of "I don't want to be here" on her face.

After about six months, my daughter began to open up to the therapist. She accepted the therapy and threw herself into learning the skills. DBT is a skills-based form of Cognitive Behavior Therapy (CBT). The patient acquires the skills to deal with certain life situations. It is close-ended – meaning, once the skills are acquired and mastered, the therapy ends. It took about eighteen months for that to happen with my daughter.

It also encourages the family members to acquire a certain set of skills that can aid in the patient's day-to-day interaction with people who are close. This includes parents, partners and siblings. So, I also participated in the therapy and learned the skills to effectively interact with my daughter. Since I'm the kind of person who does things fully, I decided to change my behavior and master the skills that were taught.

I practiced the skills in each interaction with my daughter and with other people with whom I came into contact. I did additional research and bounced ideas off of my friends in the Internet community. I adjusted the presentation of the skills as to more effectively communicate their efficacy with others.

I also noticed that the set of skills that I had acquired and that I had made second nature in my life were diametrically opposed to some of the skills that were being promoted by the self-help books I had originally read. These books were not only wrong; they were at some level harmful.

Because of this, I decided to write a book. To relay my experiences and what I'd learned during previous three years. Suffice it to say though, I didn't set out to develop a passive income, that just followed my publication and promotion of the book.

If you want more information about the history behind my development as an author and why I decided to write a book at all, I provide much more detail in my most popular book: *When Hope is Not Enough: a how-to guide for living with and loving someone with Borderline Personality Disorder.*

Anyway, I'd found a subject that I was passionate about, had first-hand experience about and knowledgeable about. Additionally, at the time there were not too many books in the space. Now, there are many more and some of them are decidedly more helpful than those that existed when I published the book in 2008.

Ask yourself: is there anything that you're passionate about? Is there anything that you have experience in? Is there anything that you are knowledgeable about?

The best-selling and most royalty generating books seem to have some passion and knowledge behind them. This is especially true with self-published books. I'll discuss various ways to self-publish a book on the Internet later in this chapter. Since I only have experience with books, I can't discuss song publishing or some of the other properties that generate royalties.

Picking a subject through market analysis

If there's nothing that you feel passionate about and you are willing to do a bit of research, you can analyze the market. What you will want to analyze is essentially:

1. **The popularity of a particular subject or category.** Are there enough readers to bother creating a property in that space? If your niche is so completely narrow, you will not be able to generate enough sales to get noticeable passive income from the property. All your invested time could be wasted.

2. **The income potential of a particular subject or category.** This is related to popularity, but it's not exactly the same. The reason that it's different is the average cost of the properties in a particular space. Some books, like textbooks, are very expensive. Some are very cheap. Even the electronic editions of textbooks can be quite expensive. While it is unlikely that you're going to be writing a college-level textbook, you might be writing a technical book, on programming or computer technology. These are typically more expensive than pulp crime fiction.

3. **The competition in a particular subject or category.** Some categories may be both popular and have a very strong income potential, yet still be difficult to penetrate. If the category is very crowded, there might not be room to break through to the consumer.

Of course, when I wrote my first book, I didn't consider any of the above market conditions. I did have a sense that there was little competition, because there were really only two or three books on the subject at the time. Now, there are many more. If I had had a market-driven reason for writing that book, I might think twice about it at this time. The competition is very strong in my book's categories. Of course, I was writing to help other people who were in the same boat as I was and I didn't consider the competition.

Additionally, I was not concerned with income potential. While my book sells many fewer than others in my category, it sells better that most. The Kindle edition sells about two to three copies a day. Most self-published Kindle book authors would be delighted at that level of sales volume because most Kindle books sell two or three copies a month. However, there are exceptions. One way to create an exception is through market analysis.

As the subtitle of this book suggests, I stumbled into the royalty game. I certainly dreamed that my first book would become a best seller and out-sell the books that were on the market in my category. Of course, I had no sense of "category" at the time. I still had no idea how to position my book or anything like that. I just wanted my book to get in front of people like me and people I could help.

To tell you the truth, I did pretty much everything wrong. I'll talk about my mistakes and what I should have done later in this chapter. That being said, I have since learned a thing or two about market analysis when it comes to generating royalties.

I currently use a tool called "Kindle Spy" which helps to analyze the Kindle sales, market conditions and competition of a particular category. While I don't specifically write or commission (see below) books fitting into particular categories, I do look at the individual categories to see how to position my work. If a category like Self-Help->Love and Relationships has a better market position than Non-Fiction->Interpersonal Relationships, I'll categorize my book in the better category. Kindle Spy helps me position the book into the most lucrative category.

Kindle Spy is a market analysis tool that specifically targets the Amazon Kindle marketplace. It essentially analyzes a particular category or search string to see how that particular category stacks up on the three factors mentioned above within the Kindle marketplace. You can purchase a copy of Kindle Spy at my companion resource Internet site in the resources section: howtomakemoneyinyourpjs.com.

There are other marketplaces other than the Amazon Kindle marketplace. I will discuss each of the ones with which I am familiar in the next section.

Life events essentially pushed me toward my subject matter with little market analysis. For you, you can start afresh and analyze the market and niche before you put in the effort to write a two hundred page book.

Writing a two hundred page book is no small undertaking, especially if you have a full-time job. I wrote my first book, which is 185 pages, on a commuter train to and from New York City. I spent 45 minutes each way and it took me several months to finish the book.

It probably would have been better if I had analyzed the marketplace before putting in all that effort – yet for me it was about the passion for the subject.

What if I don't care and just want to generate cash?

This is a valid question. You might not care about anything enough or feel confident enough to want to write a book about any subject. There is a more, in my opinion, cynical way to go about getting access to passive royalty income.

That way is through hiring a freelancer to author the book and putting your name (or pseudonym) on the book. While I haven't done this myself yet (I write all of my own material), I know people who have taken this route.

The best way that I've seen to commission a book for which you can collect royalties is through a site like eLance.com or freelancer.com. Again, I have not used either of these sites thus far. I can't recommend one or the other or an entirely different site.

The freelancers on each of these sites seem to charge either an hourly rate (around $20-30 an hour as of this writing) or a flat rate based on the size of the project ($250-750 based on a "small project"). In order to go this route you will need some upfront cash.

My friends who have commissioned ghostwritten books usually come up with the subject and the outline for the book, along with a writing sample or some sample chapters. If you choose to go this route, you will have to communicate with the freelancer to understand the requirements that will be placed upon you, the scope of the project and how to efficiently use the freelancer's time.

Even if you're writing the book yourself, it is sometimes advisable to get a copy editor to proofread the book before publication.

If you do your market research and find a category in which the competition is relatively low and the income potential and popularity are high, you can create an outline and sample chapter for that category and hire a freelancer to actually write the book.

It's a fine go-to-market strategy for developing a royalty income, but it will require some upfront cash.

How to Produce a Royalty-Generating Work

Now that you've chosen a subject for your work, no matter what method you decided upon, you have to actually produce the work. I'm going to go through the method that I follow and mention some other methods that might be better for you.

I publish what the publishing industry calls "trade" books. There are other types of books (like "mass market"), but I stick with trade books. Trade books are typically six inches wide by nine inches tall. The thickness of the book depends on how many pages are inside. I like my books to be at least 100 pages, because that thickness allows the title to be printed on the spine of the book. Less than about 100 pages, depending on the thickness of the paper, you can't print the title on the spine of the book. You will want the book to be able to have the title printed on the spine so that if your book eventually makes it into libraries (one of mine has) or book stores (a pretty difficult task), people can read the title by pursuing the shelves.

Using a Template

I start with a template. The template I use is a 6 X 9 inch trade publication template for Microsoft Word. I downloaded the template in MS-Word 2003 format from Lulu.com which is the service I use to publish my books. I will make this template available to the purchasers of this book on the resource Internet site (howtomakemoneyinyourpjs.com).

It is a custom page size. To make sure you have the proper template in place for a trade publication, just open the template, and go to Print. Word should show the "custom size (6 X 9 inches)" in the Print section of the screen.

I have modified the template by adding a title page, a copyright page and a place for the ISBN. The ISBN is the "International Standard Book Number" and is required if you want to publish a physical copy of your book through an Internet retailer like Amazon. It is not required if you want to publish the book electronically only (even on the Kindle) or if you want to sell it only on the publisher's site.

I recommend getting an ISBN for all your materials, because having more than one revenue stream (i.e. Electronic and physical) is always better than a single stream. While most of the sales of my most successful book (*When Hope is Not Enough*) are electronic, via the Kindle Store, about 25% of the sales come from physical copies of the book.

You should also choose a readable font. For the interior text of your book, you should use a "serif" font. Serif fonts are the ones that have the little pointy ends on them (like Garamond, New Times Roman and Georgia) and are not "rounded" (like Arial, Calibri and Verdana). The rounded fonts are called sans serif fonts. The general rule in type setting is that headlines or large-type words use sans serif fonts, while type in books and newspapers use serif fonts.

If you've never heard of this "rule" check out a tabloid newspaper, like the *New York Post*, and you will notice that the 96 point headlines are in a sans serif font, while the articles are printed in a serif font. Why is this the case? Typesetters have long thought that serif fonts are easier to read when the type is set close together.

You should make a place for a title page, a copyright page and for a table of contents. The title page should be the first page of the document and should include the ISBN at the bottom. The copyright page should be the next page, with a copyright notice at the bottom of this page. I don't dedicate any of my books, but the dedication page should be next and it should be blank on the back. The table of contents comes next can it can be automatically generated from the contents of the book, if need be. Finally, the first chapter should start on the first odd (right side) page.

Your book should have an even number of pages and if it doesn't you will need to include a blank page at the back of your book so the printer can produce an even number of pages. Why? Because books are printed on both sides of the paper and you must have an even number of pages to cover each side of each page. The text should also be justified; meaning, it should appear like a block of text, even on both the left and right side of each paragraph.

My template will take care of all that you need to do format-wise to produce a book.

Details about a Trade Book

As I said earlier, the trade book should be at least 100 pages such that you can have the title of the book (and the author's name) on the spine of the book. Again, a trade book is 6 inches by 9 inches in size. Normally, the trade books are printed on cream colored pages in black and white. You can print in color (if need be), but that will incur additional printing costs. If you choose to, you can print your book on white paper, rather than on cream, and you should do so if you're printing in color. I usually choose trade, cream paper and black and white printing.

Typically, a trade publication will have about 400 words on each page, taking into account the spacing, chapter headings and paragraph breaks. That means that you need to write about 30-40,000 words to get to 100 pages. My book, *When Hope is Not Enough*, is 185 pages (with a blank page at the end to make it even) and contains about 72,000 words.

In order to finish a book in a timely fashion, I typically write about 3,000 words a day, or 10-12 pages a day. That means that in less than a month, I can bang out a trade book of 100 pages. If you can keep to this sort of pace (or faster), good for you. It's not an easy pace (for me) to keep up with.

I'm not going to tell you how to write a trade book, because that's up to you. However, typically non-fiction trade books have the following characteristics:

- An Introduction – in which you outline the purpose, audience and say a thing or two about the motivation and your credentials on the subject matter.

- About 8-12 Chapters – in which you outline and explain the problem, your solution and how to go about implementing your solution in the reader's life.

If you follow the above structure of a trade publication, you should be able to knock one out in less than a month. You should also break your content up into digestible bits and not have huge blocks of text.

You should write a description of the book that uses the keywords that a person searching for a book would use. You should also title the book using keywords that will help a person find your book. I'll talk more about titles and descriptions (and covers) in the "After You've Finished the Book" section later in this chapter.

Publishing a Physical Book Yourself

There are a number of services through which you can self-publish a book. I personally use Lulu, which has been around a long time and which I used to publish a book back in 2001, although that book is no longer available. Lulu is a print-on-demand service, which means they print each book as the books are purchased. An incomplete list of print-on-demand book publishers:

- Lulu
- Create Space (owned by Amazon)
- Blurb
- Lightning Source (owned by mega-distributor Ingram)
- Wordclay

Each of these publishers has different terms of engagement, with some requiring a setup fee, some requiring no money up front. Since I've used Lulu for many years, I really only know about that service, but I have dabbled with Create Space and it seems to work generally the same way.

Neither Lulu nor Create Space requires a setup fee. They make their money by taking a cut of the overall cost of the book and by charging printing costs. An example of using Lulu to publish a trade book with the following attributes (at the time of this writing):

Book Type: Premium Paperback (Book Store Quality)
Length: 150 pages

Type: Trade Publication (6 X 9 in.)
Cover: Glossy
Page Color: Cream
Paper Quality: 60# (heaviness)
Binding: Perfect Bound (not coil-bound or saddle-stitched)

The costs for such a book with Lulu are:

Setup Fee: $0
Printing Costs: $4.25 per book (3 cents a page)
Binding Cost: $4.50 per book in non-retail, $1.50 for retail
Base Price: $8.75 for non-retail, $5.75 for retail

These prices are approximate. So, in order for you to make any money on this book, you have to charge more than $8.75 for non-retail sales (like on Lulu itself) and more than $11.50 at retail stores (like Amazon).

Wait a minute! Why $11.50 and not $5.75? That's because a retailer essentially doubles the base wholesale price ($5.75) and takes half as the retail cut of a book. You heard me right. The retailer takes half.

If I use my longest and most successful book as an example, it has exactly the same attributes of the above theoretical book, except it has 186 pages. So the costs/royalties are as follows:

Full Retail Price: $19.95
Base Price (Printing & Binding): $5.12
Net Profit: $14.83
Retailer Share: $9.97
Lulu Share (20% of Net after Retailer Share): $0.97
My Royalty: $3.88

Every time I sell a physical copy of that book through a retailer, I receive a $3.88 royalty.

When you use a print-on-demand service, the end product can end up being pricey when sold in retail outlets (including Amazon). This is because the cost of manufacturing a single book is more on a per unit basis than manufacturing a large number.

I've gotten some negative reviews on the Internet because of the cost of my book in retail. But it ultimately is what it is. If you have a valuable message that speaks to the problems of the reader, paying a little extra will not faze the reader much. As long as they get $19.95 of value from my book (and most of my readers get much more value in the long run), the reader is usually pretty happy.

Services like Lulu have a "wizard" on their publishing website that will walk you through the publishing process. This step-by-step publishing application will assign your physical book an ISBN, allow you to upload a PDF or Word document, convert your text to a book-ready format, allow you to add book details (such as description, category and keywords) and enable you to design a cover.

These services require that you order one of your own books before you're allowed to release the book for distribution. While this will cost you the base price of the book plus the service's royalty cut (for my book, it's $4.87 plus tax and shipping), it's a good idea that they do this. It gives you an opportunity to hold the physical book in your hands and to give it a good read-through. It helps to eliminate pagination weirdness that can occur during a conversion from source documents to print-ready format. It also helps to eliminate typos and formatting errors. Even though I ended up buying eight copies of my book the first time, it was well worth it. I continued to make revisions to the book throughout those eight times and had to buy a new copy with each revision.

That said, I still had typos and errors in the text. I think with most self-published books you're going to have to live with those. It's almost impossible (for me anyway) to eliminate all typos and grammatical mistakes.

Yet, once you've written a royalty producing product, you have enabled a passive revenue stream that didn't exist before.

After You've Finished the Book

Once you've finished creating a royalty producing book, there are some tasks that you'll need to perform to get it to market. I basically did most of these tasks wrong when I published my first book. Hopefully, you can learn from my mistakes and not repeat them yourself.

Proof Reading and Editing

As I said above, the publisher will require you to buy an initial copy of your book before it is available to the public. I would suggest that you read through the book yourself and have someone else read it as well. I actually did do this with my first book and it was very helpful. However, I made additional changes to the book without having a third party read through and approve of the changes. This introduced errors in the book.

If you're going to make changes to the copy in the book after it has been read by a third party, I'd suggest you have the third party read through the book again to insure that you're not introducing errors in your book.

There are also some applications available online to electronically proofread your book. One application that I use is called Ginger, which will proofread your copy and suggest grammatical changes, corrections and rephrasing. There are other such applications available to you for online, electronic or application-based proofreading. You should probably Google "electronic proofreading" and get an idea of the applications that are available.

Choosing a Cover

This is another area in which I made a mistake. I was so anxious to publish my book, *When Hope is Not Enough,* that I just chose a solid cover (green) with simple yellow type on the front. There is nothing on the back of the cover. While it has sort of become known as "the little green book" in the community that has grown up around it, the cover really shows that it is self-published and not fully professional. It would have been much better if I'd chosen a high resolution photograph and uploaded it to act as the cover. Perhaps I will have to put out a second edition of the book with a new cover.

The publishing company that you use will likely have a "cover wizard" for building a more professional-looking cover. These cover templates are fine and look more professional than the solid color and simple text on my book's cover, but you can fall victim to having a cover very similar to other authors also using the cover wizard.

If you chose to make the cover yourself from a photograph, there are some considerations. You have to own the license/copyright on the photograph. You can purchase a stock photo from a service like iStockphoto, but that can get expensive as you will need world-wide rights to a high resolution version of the photograph. You will also need to edit the photograph to include the title of your book. The publishing service will likely have a template for editing in a program like Photoshop that can guide you through the creation of a professional-looking cover. If you go the single photograph route, this is called a "wrap around" cover. There will be a little rectangle on the back where the bar code needs to appear.

There are some free stock photo services; however, many of these restrict usage of the photos in a print-on-demand setting. Also, many of the photos available from a free stock photo service are of web quality (72 dpi) whereas you will need a higher resolution version of a photo for your book cover, typically 300 or more dots per inch (dpi).

I'd say you want your cover to look professional and the most professional look is the wraparound cover, but if you do not have the skills to pull that off, use the cover wizard to create a cover for your book.

Writing a Book Description

You will need to write a brief description of the book. This description is very important! I didn't realize how important the description was until I saw how it was used. Your description will be used anywhere the book is to be sold, either on the publisher's site or at a retail establishment like Amazon. It follows your book wherever it goes. It is important that your description speak to the potential readers of your book.

The description I wrote for my book is OK. It's not perfect in that I didn't really consider the keywords that a potential reader would be searching on to locate my book. Amazon is essentially a large search engine for books and eBooks (along with many other products). One factor that affects people's ability to find your book is the description (and also the title and subtitle).

Search engine optimization (SEO) is a process in which people who are publishing on the web associate certain keywords with their websites and webpages. While a long discussion of SEO is beyond the scope of this book, some level of SEO can take place within your description. You should use keywords that identify your reader's concerns.

Keywords and Categories

The publishers (at least Lulu) allow you to assign keywords to your book. These seem helpful but they don't serve too much purpose outside of the publisher's website. They do offer some guidance and will direct people using Google toward you book, but only on the publisher's website.

Retailers like Amazon will not use these keywords. Once your book is up and selling through Amazon, the keywords will not benefit you much.

Categories, on the other hand, come in two forms: publisher's categories and retailer's categories. The publisher's categories, which you can assign at the publisher's website, provide guidance about your book to shoppers on the publisher's website. They also get translated into retailer's categories for a printed book. For example, if you choose "self-help" as the category for your book at the publisher's website, the printed book will be placed in the self-help section of the retailer's website.

You are likely to have many more sales from a retailer (even if the royalty is lower) than from the publisher's site. The "page rank" (Google's measure for the relevancy and popularity of a website) is going to make it such that the retailer's site will appear in a search above the publisher.

Once the book is available on a service like Amazon, you should focus on Amazon more than on the publisher's site. People search things more often through Google than they browse the "shelves" of a print-on-demand publisher. So, your readers are more likely to get exposure to your work on Amazon than the publisher's website since the page rank of Amazon is going to be much higher than other websites. When people search on Google, Amazon is more likely to show up at the top of an organic (not paid) results list.

Creating an Excerpt

You should also create an excerpt that can be read without purchasing the book. I usually have a 15-20 page excerpt for my books. These are available for reading both at the publisher's site as well as within the "Look Inside" feature on Amazon. This allows your potential readers to see the table of contents, the introduction and a bit of the content of the book itself. If you do a good job of engaging your readers in the Introduction, an excerpt can go a long way to getting sales.

Publishing an eBook

EBooks come in various forms and are published in various formats. The traditional downloadable eBook is a PDF, sometimes a protected PDF, sometimes not. The physical, print-on-demand services offer electronic publishing services as well. There are a variety of considerations when publishing to a particular format. For my books I have placed my bets on the Kindle Platform and I'll give you additional details on what that means in a little while. However, the most common and lucrative formats and distribution methods are (from least lucrative to most – for me):

- PDF publishing distributed through the publisher or self-distributed.
- Nook (ePub) publishing distributed through Barnes & Noble platform.
- ePub publishing distributed through the iStore (Apple) platform.
- Kindle publishing distributed through Amazon's Kindle Book Store.

PDF Publishing

Publishing eBooks as PDFs is what pretty much every electronic publisher did before Apple released the iStore and Amazon released the Kindle. It's still a viable publishing option today. Lulu gives you to option to selling a PDF version of your self-published book at their site. When you create a physical book, you can also choose to sell an eBook in the PDF format.

PDF readers are available on many platforms including computers, tablets and other mobile devices. Amazon's Kindle application and device will read PDFs.

However, my experience has been that the eBook as a PDF for sale's time has passed. Although I was selling a handful of eBooks as PDFs a month when I utilized this format, I found that other formats, such as Kindle and iBooks were selling far better than PDFs, starting about two to three years ago.

There was a time, about 5 years ago when I sold my books in PDF format directly to the public using the Google Checkout process to collect money and to auto-distribute the material or a password to unlock the download of the material. I discontinued this when New York State (where I live) started charging sales taxes for materials sold on the Internet to New York State residents. I just didn't want to have to deal with the headache of reporting and paying sales taxes to the state of New York. I mean, suddenly my passive income got way less passive, and I was forced to deal with a government entity – too much of a pain for too little gain.

While you can make some income from selling PDFs through the publisher (like Lulu), there are now other considerations, detailed below, that play a factor in the efficacy of the PDF format.

I still believe that the PDF format is good for downloadable samples of my books, for complex eBooks that require color pictures and/or diagrams and for free eBooks that pull a reader into your wider array of offerings. I publish a free 25 page eBook in PDF format that is downloadable from my blog site. The purpose of this free eBook is to familiarize my potential readers with my philosophy and approach toward my subject matter. It serves as a "teaser" and a marketing tool for the paid products I produce. PDF is a good format for these purposes, because this free book is attractive, with many color illustrations to ease in the understanding of the concepts I'm attempting to convey.

Although Lulu still offers me opportunity to sell my books as PDF eBooks, I no longer sell PDF versions of my books for another reason, which I will explain in the section on the Kindle distribution platform below.

ePub Nook eBook Publishing

Barnes and Noble once ran an eBook self-publishing site called Pubit! In 2013, Barnes and Noble phased out Pubit! and replaced it with Nook Press, which was meant to compete with Amazon's Kindle Direct Publishing platform (about which I will talk about at length in a little while).

When I first published my first book, I thought it would be most advantageous to publish eBooks on every platform, so I published on the Pubit!/Nook platform as well as others, including PDF. However, I found that the Nook platform just didn't drive enough sales.

I ended up making only about $50 in royalties from the Nook platform over three years. It just wasn't enough to justify the fact that publishing on the Nook platform froze me out of some other markets. I decided last year to retire the Nook version of my books.

ePub iStore eBook Publishing

Apple's iStore accepts the ePub format just like the Nook store. You can have you book converted to this format through the publisher's site (i.e.

Lulu's site). I'm not certain if Amazon's Create Space also provides this facility. Given that Apple and Amazon are bitter rivals when it comes to eBooks, I doubt that this is an option from an Amazon-owned company.

I used to sell my eBooks through the iStore and I actually received quite a bit of revenue from the Apple distribution method. When I was selling eBooks through Lulu and distributing through Apple's iStore, I was receiving approximately 7% of my income through the iStore. It was a significant amount.

With as many Apple devices available in the world (including hundreds of millions of iPhones), the iStore is a great channel for making passive income.

If your publisher does not offer a conversion to ePub format for distribution in the iStore (or full distribution in the iStore), you can convert the book yourself via a number of online services or downloadable applications. If you Google "conversion to ePub" you'll be directed to a number of them.

Kindle Direct Publishing

The most lucrative channel for me has been Kindle Direct Publishing (kdp.amazon.com). Rather than have Lulu convert my books to Kindle editions, I went directly to Amazon's Kindle Direct Publishing and published my books as Kindle books.

Amazon's Kindle platform has revolutionized the eBook industry. There are millions of Kindle devices and Kindle applications installed throughout the world. The Kindle application runs on Apple's iOS, Android devices as well as on computers and within browsers. There is a downloadable version from Google Play and the iStore. There is a Chrome plugin in which you can read your Kindle books within the Chrome browser. There is also a downloadable application that runs on PCs and on Macintosh computers. Amazon uses the "whisper sync" protocol to sync your Kindle library across the Kindle applications and devices.

There are a number of different purchasing options within the Kindle Store. There are also some royalty options as well. Depending on the country and region, you can receive either a 70% or 35% royalty on your Kindle books. The nice thing about Kindle Direct Publishing is that if you choose your royalty level appropriately, you can sell your book world-wide. I've had sales from the UK, Canada, Australia, India, Japan, France and other countries throughout the world.

The format for the Kindle is not ePub as with some other services. It is a scaled down version of HTML, converted to a format very similar to the "Mobipocket" format. Unlike straight HTML, the format doesn't support many of the tags.

The Mobipocket format (aka .mobi) can be directly read into Amazon's Kindle Direct Publishing application. While Kindle Direct Publishing can also read PDFs and other files, I prefer to provide my books in the mobi format. There are a couple of reasons for this. One is that you can embed the cover image into the file. This means that when a person downloads the Kindle book onto the Kindle device or application, the cover of the book will appear both in their library and in the book itself. Secondly, the mobi format allows for page breaks and other format control (such as text size) that an uploaded PDF would support. I've found that uploaded PDFs convert poorly to Kindle format. The "end" format is called AZW (or ASW3 for newer Kindle devices) which is Amazon's slight modification to the mobi format. However, Kindle Direct Publishing will do the conversion from the mobi file to ASW.

I use a tool to convert my books to a Kindle-ready format. What I do is I first write the book in MS Word (using my template) and then I save the book in the "Web Page, Filtered" format. This will create a simple HTML version of my document. Unfortunately, Microsoft in their wisdom includes some tags that are not supported in the mobi format (like certain stylesheets and font tags). I then open the HTML file in the mobi converter (I use a convertor called Calibre). I add the cover photo and save.

Once the eBook is in mobi format, it can be uploaded to Kindle Direct Publishing and published on the Kindle platform. There are a number of options when publishing a book for the Kindle.

The basic options for a Kindle book are:

- Title
- Subtitle (optional)
- Part of a Series? (optional)
- Edition Number (optional)

- Publisher (optional)
- Description (important!)
- Book contributors
- Language
- ISBN (optional and it should NOT be the same as the physical book)
- Verify your publishing rights (either public domain or you own it)
- Categories (important!)
- Age Range (optional)
- US Grade Range (optional)
- Keywords (important – but not as important as categories)
- Release (either now or pre-order)
- Book Cover File (shown on Amazon's webpages)
- Digital Right Management (DRM prevents the book from being shared)
- Upload book content (the mobi file)

I usually don't select "Digital Rights Management." I like my readers to have the ability to share the books or give them as gifts, which you can only do if DRM is turned off.

Kindle Select

There is one other option, which has to do with Kindle Select. Kindle Select is an Amazon program that allows Kindle Users who have Amazon Prime to check out Kindle books like a library. It's actually called Kindle Online Lending Library (KOLL). A Kindle user can borrow your book and it remains on the Kindle for a period of time and then disappears. Your book has to be enrolled in Kindle Select for readers to have access to it in KOLL.

Amazon also introduced a new program called Kindle Unlimited (or KU). This program allows Kindle users to pay a monthly fee to have access to Kindle Select books for free. Basically, it's the same as KOLL without the expiration date.

In order for your book to be available to KOLL and Kindle Unlimited, you have to enroll the book in Kindle Select. However, there are some restrictions on having your book in Kindle Select. The biggest restriction is that your book cannot be available in a digital format anywhere except via the Kindle Store. That means no Nook, no PDF and (most importantly) no iStore. I have had my books enrolled in Kindle Select for a while now and I'm still analyzing the opportunity and consequences of this decision.

The royalty for these KU/KOLL books is much less than for a purchased Kindle edition of your book. Amazon has a "global fund" with a certain pool of funds each month. Based on the number of units your readers accessed via KU/KOLL versus the total number of KU/KOLL units, you get a portion of that total fund. If you're in the top authors in a given month, you could also receive a bonus of up to $5,000. You also get a larger royalty share on your sold units in some markets (70% vs 35%).

I have seen many of my books read through KU/KOLL. I am hoping that it will give me more exposure for my entire library, but I'm still analyzing the issue now. I can't tell you whether to enroll in Kindle Select or not. While the Kindle application is available on Apple devices, my sales through the iStore have now ceased. It could have been a poor decision to throw my hat into the ring with Amazon's Kindle Select. Only time will tell. The good news is that the enrollment period for Kindle Select is 90 days at a time and you can remove your book from the program at any time.

Kindle Store Categories

Kindle Store Categories are very important to promoting your work. As I said earlier in this chapter, I use a product called Kindle Spy to analyze the popularity, income potential and competition of a particular category. At howtomakemoneyinyourpjs.com, I've collected all of these resources together to make it easier for you.

Kindle Spy is not free. It requires that you pay a one-time license fee. I have a link on my resources page to Kindle Spy. I will talk more about this link and how to use THAT to make money in the next chapter.

Kindle Spy allows you to do the market research in Amazon Kindle Categories in an automated way. You can navigate to potential categories and use the Chrome browser Kindle Spy plugin to analyze the category. Kindle Spy will list the best sellers in any category by the volume of sales, from best-selling to least-selling for the first 100 Kindle Books in the category. It will also provide a red/yellow/green rating of the category in terms of popularity, potential (income potential) and competition.

An example of this is the category that this book fits into. I selected Business & Money > Entrepreneurship & Small Business > Home-Based. I was lucky to find that this category is the right category for this book. At the time of this writing, all three categories – popularity, potential and competition are green. The total monthly revenue for the top 100 books in this category is more than $66,000. The average price of a Kindle Book in this category is $3.85. The top-selling book in this category sells more than 2,000 copies a month and the top revenue producing book is generating more than $13,000 a month.

These are very good numbers and all provided by Kindle Spy. When I looked at a different category like Business & Money > Entrepreneurship & Small Business > Entrepreneurship, I saw that the competition in that category was yellow, meaning the competition was greater in the category than in the Home-Based one.

Just a note: the categories in the Kindle Store are NOT the same as those in the general Amazon Bookstore. I think this is because the categories for physical books are fixed across the book retailing industry (this is why when you choose a category at the publisher, it carries over to the physical book retailer). I assume that Amazon created more detailed categories for their Kindle Store because they had complete control over the categories.

You are allowed to place your Kindle Book into up to two categories within the Kindle Store via Kindle Direct Publishing. If you look at my most popular book, *When Hope is Not Enough*, I placed it into the category Health, Fitness & Dieting > Mental Health > Mood Disorders. As of the time of this writing, the book ranks number 24 in that category. I didn't do any market research into the category before I placed the book in that category. Hell, I didn't even know you could do that!

That category has a green potential and competition, but a yellow popularity rating. I know that now. Being number 24 is something of a problem for this book. I'd like to be in the top 20 because when someone browses this category, my book is on the second page, not the first page. As far as a search on Amazon goes, my book doesn't show up in the top ten for the searches I want it to show. That again is a problem and a mistake by me regarding the title, subtitle and description of the book.

I implore you to read this entire chapter and approach the title, subtitle, description and category with care. It can make the difference between making hundreds of dollars a month or less (as I do) and making thousands of dollars a month.

Kindle Spy also shows a "word cloud" of the most popular words in the titles of the best-selling books. You can choose from some of these for the title of your book. Originally, I was going to title this book "Make Money While You Sleep" but there is another book on the same title with the same general subject.

I then considered "Stumbling Toward Cash" which reflected the inadvertent way that I approached a passive income. I really did stumble into it. However, Kindle Spy showed me that, in the Home-Based category, the most popular words in the titles and subtitles of those books were: how, make, money, your and online. I changed the title of this book to reflect those keywords.

A Note about Pricing

Pricing is a tricky subject for eBooks. The main publishers seem to price their eBook about $9.99 or more. In the iStore, my book was priced at $9.99. However, at Amazon, I have been playing around with pricing to see if changing the price changes my sales volume.

At Amazon, the minimum price for a Kindle Book is $0.99. Using Kindle Spy to gauge the average price of a Kindle Book in your chosen category is a good approach. I definitely approached my pricing in a very haphazard way.

I think that a good rule of thumb for pricing a Kindle Book is one third the cost of the printed edition, if that printed edition is self-published through a print-on-demand publishing service. My book costs $19.95 for a printed copy. I had originally priced my Kindle Book at $7.50, which is about 37% of the printed cost. However, I lowered the cost of $6.99 which is closer to one third (35%) of the retail, printed price.

If you're publishing on Kindle-only, I suggest that the price of your book should be below $4.00. Looking at the prices of books in the Home-Based category, the average price is below $4.00 and the prices range from $0.99 to more than $15.00. Most of the books are in the $3.00 range.

Amazon also runs campaigns for Kindle Books under $4.00. In order to have your Kindle Book included in one of those campaigns, you obviously have to make the book price below $4.00.

Discounts and Promotions

Lulu, the print-on-demand publisher I use, provides the ability for the author of the book to offer a discount off the retail price. If you sell your book directly from the publisher, rather than from a retail site like Amazon, your royalty will be much higher per sale. My royalty from selling a book on Lulu is $12.06 per book, while my retail royalty is $3.88. As you can see it's more than three times greater than selling on Amazon. While I'd like to have everyone buy the printed book at Lulu, I sell a larger majority on Amazon. In March of 2015, I sold only two printed copies through Lulu and sold over 50 copies from various Amazon sites (US, UK and Canada). I sold a handful through Ingram, which is the book publishing service that provides libraries and book stores.

Even though the royalty is much higher on a copy sold through Lulu, my readers are buying mostly through Amazon. That's just the reality of the situation.

The reason I'm bringing the sales volumes up in a section about discounts is that I have the ability to deeply discount my book at Lulu to lure sales. I cannot affect the Amazon price of my printed book. It's something of a mystery as to how Amazon prices printed books. The price of my book fluctuates from the retail price that I set ($19.95) and a lower amount (typically about $17.96). I have no insight to their pricing and discounting methodology. I have no control over it.

I do have control over the discounts available at Lulu. Since my royalty is $12.06 at Lulu and $3.88 at Amazon, I can discount the book up to $8.17 (about 40%) and still receive a greater royalty for books sold at Lulu. Once your book gains some traction in the marketplace, you should consider running some discounted periods and marketing these to your readers.

There are also some discount programs available within Kindle Direct Publishing. I've already discussed the Kindle Select program, which is something of a discount program for Amazon Prime (for Kindle Online Lending Library) and Kindle Unlimited members. However, there are some other discount programs that Amazon offers that can benefit your royalty stream.

The first discount program is called Kindle Countdown Deal. It essentially allows you to create a discounted price for a particular period of time. You can lower the price and have that price cover a particular time period. This discount method is intended to "create excitement" around the book.

The second discount program is called Free Book Promotion. It allows you to offer a book for free for a period of time. I did this with one of my lesser-selling books, *Beyond Boundaries*, for a period of five days. I had over 200 readers download the free version of the book. My intention was to push people toward my other, better-selling books. Did it work? I'm not sure. My sales didn't really go up right after the promotion. However, I did get a book of mine into the hands of several hundred people who would not otherwise read it. Free is good sometimes!

Selling a Physical Book via a Marketplace

Since as the author of your book, you receive a greatly discounted price when you buy a copy directly from the publisher, you can act as a reseller of your own book and make money on the margin. I put this method in this book because it is viable, but it is NOT passive. You have to manage this carefully.

The idea here is that you buy a number of copies of your physical book from the publisher. My cost of my physical book is $4.87 at Lulu. If I bought, say, 10 copies of the book, it would cost me $4.87 plus tax and shipping. Please don't forget about tax and shipping! Tax on an order of 10 books is $5.67 (NY Tax) and shipping by the slowest method (US Mail) is $15.24. The total cost of 10 copies of my book from Lulu is $69.61 (for me only!). That means the cost of each copy would be $6.96. That's significantly less than even the discounted price for the physical book at Amazon ($17.96).

Once you receive the copies of the book, you can sell the book on eBay or within the Amazon Marketplace. When I purused eBay, there are sellers trying to sell my book price anywhere from $18.27 to $26.66. It seems odd to me. If I wanted to, I could jump onto eBay and sell my own book for significantly less than these prices and make a profit. But again, you have to take shipping costs into account.

Within the Amazon Marketplace, sellers are attempting to sell a copy of my book for between $13.96 + shipping to $200! So, at a cost of goods (for each copy) of $6.96, I could offer my own book for sale at a much lower price than the above sellers.

But, and this is a BIG but, you will have to manage the interaction with the buyer and handle and ship the copy to the seller. That's NOT passive. It requires some work on your part and may be beyond the effort you want to expend just to make a couple of bucks. It's up to you. I did it for a while, but it required more effort than I was willing to expend.

Of course, another possibility is to sell a "personalized" copy of the book through these services. That is, a signed copy or one that contains a personal message. But again, this will require an active effort on your part.

Conclusion about Royalties

Royalties are my biggest source of passive income. They can be the greatest source of passive income for you as well. Writing a book and/or an eBook is an easy way to get into the royalty game.

You should do it with deliberation, unlike how I got into the royalty game. I stumbled in not know the ins and outs of the system. Luckily, I was able to translate my knowledge and passion into a nice royalty income stream.

Since I first wrote and published my best-selling book (and eBook), I have learned a number of things about both processes. In summary, rather than make all the mistakes that I made you should:

- Compare print-on-demand publishers for the cost of setup and per-copy charge.
- Create a book of at least 100 pages so the title can be printed on the spine of the book (perfect bound).
- Research the category in which your book is likely to live. Make sure that the category is favorable in terms of popularity, income potential and competition.
- Research key words to include in your title, subtitle and description.
- Use a pre-formatted template.
- Choose a professional cover.
- Proofread.
- Price your book appropriately.

- Monitor your channels to see which is most effective and focus on that one.
- Look to my resource site to get access to some of this analysis and tools (howtomakemoneyinyourpjs.com)

If you follow these guidelines for creating a royalty-based product, you should be much more ahead of the game than I was when I started. You should be able to avoid the mistakes I made. Hopefully, if you have your book appropriately positioned as outlined in this book, you should see a passive revenue stream in short order.

A final note about royalties: royalties are typically paid in a "trailing" manner. This means that royalties are paid either 30 or 60 days after they are earned. This is to monitor returns. Once the return period ends, your royalty will be paid. Some entities will pay quarterly.

Chapter 2: Affiliate Income

The second most lucrative channel for me is Affiliate Income. Being an affiliate for a product, service or feature of an Internet-based retailer or other service provider is sort of like being an outside marketing and sales arm of the entity. There are thousands of affiliate programs on the Internet in every conceivable category of goods and services.

I am a member of a number of different affiliate programs. However, in order to receive affiliate income, you have to have some sort of Internet presence - a blog, a website or an affiliate-generated page. I will explain how I created my website and blog, which provide affiliate links to generate income.

If you Google "affiliate programs" you are bound to find hundreds of programs available for you to enroll in. There are as wide-ranging as travel, web hosting, fitness, debt relief, insurance, even private jets. I am personally a member of several affiliate programs. There are also affiliate aggregators like (formerly) Commission Junction (now Affiliate by Conversant), LinkShare, Clickbank and ShareASale. There are others that specialize in certain types of products, like JVZoo and others.

There are also affiliate programs run by the largest companies on the Internet, such as Amazon, Apple, Expedia, Trip Advisor, Priceline and others.

The way an affiliate program works is this:

1. You sign up for the affiliate program, providing your tax ID (either social security number or business EIN).
2. Some affiliate programs require acceptance and approval of the merchant.
3. Once you are approved (if required), the affiliate program will provide you with a set of formatted links or an affiliate ID to include in your links to the product or service.
4. You promote the product or service on your affiliate site and include the formatted links to the affiliated product or service.
5. Once someone purchases the product or service after following the link from your website, you receive a commission on the sale.

Commission Rates

Commission rates range wildly between affiliates. Some affiliate sites have "tiered" rates, the more you sell, the more you make.

I'd like to examine a couple of example affiliate commission rates such that you can get an understanding of how these work.

Amazon Associates

Amazon has a multi-tiered commission system across their various stores, programs and sales channels. Amazon also has several different programs that can be considered "affiliate programs". The one I'm going to examine is Amazon Associates, which is the "pure affiliate" program. It allows you to sell books, DVDs, electronics and many other offerings from Amazon.

Basically, you can join Amazon Associates without approval. Amazon has two types of commission plans: fixed based on product type or tiered based on sales volume of "general products". I personally get more out of the tiered system because I typically only link to books from my blog site (details to follow).

I do, however, get some "downstream" sales. What that means is that a person browsing my blog site will click on an affiliate link, such as one of my recommended books from the recommended reading list, and will either buy the book or continue shopping on Amazon and buys something else. The affiliate ID on the link will follow this person around during their time on Amazon if the link originated from my blog site. I get a commission on any sale of any item as long as my affiliate ID is associated with the original link. To me, that's a downstream commission.

For example, my blog site (which I'll talk about in more detail later in this chapter) lists mainly books and eBooks for sale on Amazon. I have created a recommended reading list for the consumers of my blog. In a typical month, I will end up selling about 50 items through the affiliate program. Since my linked items are not very expensive, the total commission on these items is usually between $50-100 per month. As for the downstream sales, last month I sold a "Mega Bloks Ride On Caterpillar with Excavator" in the category of Toys & Games. I can assure you, that item is NOT linked on my blog site! I sold nine items (out of 62 last month) in this manner. It's just a nice side effect of having an Amazon Associates site.

Now let's analyze the commission structures for product categories and the general products.

Fixed Commission for Product Categories

As of this writing, Amazon offers a fixed commission schedule for certain product categories. It is subject to change at any time, so I can't assure you the fixed commission schedule will remain in this form.

Fixed Advertising Fee Rates for Specific Product Categories

- Electronics – 4.00%
- Kindle tablets, readers and Fire phone – 4.00%
- Amazon Echo and Fire TV – 7.00%
- Amazon MP3 Product – 5.00%
- Amazon Instant Video Products – 5.00%
- Game Download Products – 10.00%
- Gift Cards redeemable at Amazon – 6.00%
- Gift Cards not redeemable at Amazon – 4.00%
- Amazon Coins – 10.00%
- Grocery Items – 4.00%
- Video Game Console Products – 1.00%
- Headphone Products – 6.00%
- DVD Products – 4.00%
- Industrial Products – 8.00%
- Products available on Myhabit.com – 8.00%
- Products available on Amazon Local – 6.00%

Tiered Commission for General Products

The tiered commission system is between 4-8.5% of the sale, based on volume. If you sell more than a certain number of items in a particular month, your sales commission increases. The mechanics of using Amazon Associates will be covered later in this chapter, but first I'd like to look at the commission structure in more detail and let you know how much money you can expect from the channel. As I said, in a typical month, I sell about 50-60 items from the links that I provide on my blog site and the downstream sales.

At the time of this writing, the commission structure within Amazon Associates for general products looks like this:

Number of Items – Commission

- 1-6 items – 4.00%
- 7-30 items – 6.00%
- 31-110 items – 6.50%
- 111-320 items – 7.00%
- 321-630 items – 7.50%
- 631-1570 items – 8.00%
- 1571-3130 items – 8.25%
- 3131+ items – 8.50%

Although my average commission fluctuates for different products and in different categories, it ranges between 5.05%-6.53% for the products I sell. On products that have an average price of $11.65 (removing the Ride On Caterpillar Toy, which costs $43.99), the commission on each sale is about $0.76. Not enough to make me filthy rich, but every little bit helps.

Because of the way, when I got into the business of passive income creation, I did no analysis on what would be the most lucrative approach to Amazon Associates income. I just linked books that I had read and enjoyed and thought would be helpful to my readers, including my own books.

However, you can do some analysis on what product category or sales strategy you would want to use to take full advantage of the Amazon Associates program. While mine was completely related to the subject of my books, yours doesn't have to be (although if it is, you can build toward the most lucrative passive income channel covered in a later chapter of this book). You can choose to use a strategy with a completely different approach or subject matter than your royalty-producing products.

For example, you could focus on higher priced items such that the commission would be higher on each sale. You could focus on a product category with a higher commission rate to get a higher commission on each sale. It's really up to you.

In a measure of full disclosure here, I want to look at another affiliate relationship I have. It's with the product Kindle Spy, which I described in the last chapter. Kindle Spy is a Chrome Browser Plugin that offers market analysis of Kindle Book Store Categories. I described it in much detail in the previous chapter. It is a very valuable product and I highly recommend it.

At first I was just a user of Kindle Spy. I was looking for a way to maximize my royalties for my Kindle Books. Somehow I stumbled upon Kindle Spy. I don't even remember how. It's an excellent product and at the time of this writing it costs $47.00 for a one-time license fee.

Kindle Spy was created by Wesley Atkins and he is a very aggressive marketer of passive income methods for Kindle Books. He uses JVZoo which is an Ecommerce platform for digital goods and services. JVZoo manages the sales of the product and distributes the product. They also have an affiliate program. When I discovered what a great product Kindle Spy was, after using it to do market research on various Kindle Store categories, I decided to apply as an affiliate for the product. Wesley does require that you supply him with the reason that you want to be an affiliate for his product. However, there are many other products available on JVZoo for which you can be an affiliate as well.

Kindle Spy is part of a "sales funnel" on JVZoo. It is actually the beginning of the funnel. The funnel leads to more products, services and educational materials. Essentially, once you buy Kindle Spy, you're moved through the funnel toward other services. Be prepared for a lot of marketing! I'll talk about marketing later in this book.

The reason I mention JVZoo in this section is the sales commission is much higher on most products than Amazon Associates. The commission rate for Kindle Spy is currently 60%. That's 60% of every $47 sale, or $28.20. Three sales of the product are enough for me to receive the same passive income as I receive from Amazon Associates monthly.

Why has he set the commission so high for that product? The reason is the sales funnel. He is banking on you, the affiliate, getting new customers into his sales funnel so that he can up-sell you on pricier services, especially recurring monthly subscription products and services. He also pays out a large commission on those products and services (sometimes up to 50%).

The key here is not to get you to become an affiliate of JVZoo or Kindle Spy; it's to make you aware that some affiliate programs have a much higher commission rate than others.

Choosing an Affiliate Program

Just like choosing what to write about, affiliate programs can be chosen in a variety of ways. I really had no strategy in choosing the affiliate programs and products that I would promote. Well… that's not entirely true.

How I Selected My Affiliate Programs

Many years ago, before I wrote my best-selling book and starting blogging about the subject of being a loved one of someone with Borderline Personality Disorder, I owed a fairly large number of domain names. I was a technician working for a large telecommunications company and I had access to the Internet and World Wide Web very early, in 1992 in fact. At that time, I understood the importance of Internet real estate (domain names) and, although it was much more expensive to register a domain back then, I spent a great deal of money registering a number of domains. My idea was to sell affiliate products through these domains and try to make a little money on the side. That idea didn't really work out.

What did work out for me is that I sold several of those domain names for thousands of dollars apiece.

That aside, I set up a number of affiliate accounts that related to the domains in question. Unfortunately for me, this resulted in a mish-mash of IDs, emails and affiliate accounts with no central strategy or marketing plan. That was a huge mistake on my part.

Once I had the experience with my daughter and her therapy, I educated myself on the emotional regulation component of her disorder and started sharing online on an anonymous email board. I found that many of the people at that board were not receptive to my message; in fact, most were hostile. Another user of the board suggested that I start my own email list and I did in May of 2006. I offered the service for free to interested parties, each person requiring my approval before joining. The board is still in operation today and has over 1,000 members. I offered membership at no charge because that was what was traditionally done in online support communities.

I had already started my blog (http://www.anythingtostopthepain.com) in December of 2005. I had no plan, no strategy. I was just trying to relay information that had been imparted to me and was helpful in my situation. I didn't charge anything. I had no idea that I could work the blog and the group into making money. I was clueless.

Since I did have some experience in Amazon Associates from my domain names, I added some books that were helpful to me on my blog through affiliate links to Amazon. I immediately began to make money, but not much. In my first few months of offering affiliate books to my blog's readers, I made about $10 a month.

What I discovered, and had stumbled upon, was a community of people that were desperate for answers. Since I had been communicating with the loved ones of people with Borderline Personality Disorder, I had found a niche. It was a niche that I truly cared about (and still do). It was also a group of people that were frantically seeking some sort of skills that effectively worked in their relationships. I had unknowingly patched together those skills. I had answers for these people.

After answering the same questions, again and again, on my email list (which had about 200 members at the time), for about two years, I finally decided to write a book about my experiences and my solutions to the problem. Again, I had no idea how popular the book would be. I was just writing it to point my group members to a resource such that I didn't have to answer the same questions over and over.

I published the book in 2008. I began to get noticed and get known in the community as something of an authoritative voice. So again, I had found my niche completely by accident and through the back door.

But I found this niche with passion. I was, and still am, quite passionate about this cause and the community.

Yet, in some ways, I'd backed myself into a corner. I was known only within a small community of people (which has grown five-fold in the last nine years) and the only affiliate relationships that made sense were within the community itself. That meant books on the subject of emotional skills, borderline personality disorder and other similar subjects. I have yet to find affiliate programs that will click with my audience.

While I did find a niche - albeit accidentally and by circumstances beyond my control - the niche doesn't lend itself to a wide variety of affiliate relationships. Amazon Associates is the only one that makes a whole lot of sense on my blog.

I have used Amazon Associates to sell many books and to get downstream sales, as described earlier. The way that I organize my affiliate links has been quite effective. I will describe the mechanics of this organization and the tools I use to accomplish it in the next section of this chapter.

Choosing Affiliate Relationships More Strategically

As I said in the previous section, I didn't approach my affiliate relationships strategically, because I stumbled into the subject matter by circumstance. You don't have to do that. You can approach the topic around which your affiliate relationships are built in a strategic manner.

First of all, you will want to find a niche that is like the Amazon Kindle Store categories. That is, it should be popular, have income potential and not have too much competition.

You can find out if your niche is popular and what the competition is for that niche by using the Google Keyword Planner. You have to be a member of Google's AdWords program to use this tool. Sign up is free. I'll talk about AdSense (which is Google's third party advertising system) later in this book.

When you use the Keyword Planner, you can type in key words that are relevant to your subject. The Keyword Planner will show you the number of searches that Google users run per month on those keywords. It will also show a competition rating.

When I used the Keyword Planner just now, I used the Keywords "borderline personality disorder" and found that the average number of monthly searches using that phrase was 368,000. That indicates that these words are searched on many times on Google. It also showed me that the competition for this phrase was low. The Keyword Planner will also suggest other similar keywords and rate them in several categories.

For example, the term "DBT" (which is the abbreviation for the treatment of the disorder) had 60,500 searches and the competition was low, and "bipolar disorder" had 450,000 searches, but the competition was medium.

If we turn to affiliate ideas with a higher commission than books, we might look into travel and vacation packages.

The keyword "travel" has 450,000 searches and the competition is medium. However, "cheap tickets" has 1,500,000 searches but the competition is marked as high. The keywords "travel news" have 74,000 monthly searches and low competition. If you're considering joining a travel affiliate network, where the commission can be high, it makes sense to get more specific. For example:

For Keyword – Monthly Searches – Competition

- All-inclusive resorts – 165,000 – High
- Vacation Packages – 135,000 – High
- Honeymoon Packages – 74,000 - High
- Caribbean Cruise – 74,000 - High

But for more specific niches:

- Jamaica – 673,000 – Low
- Barbados – 368,000 – Low
- Vacation to go – 33,100 – Low

If you go with a more specific niche, like "Jamaica Vacation to Go", you're likely to get more traffic with less competition for eyeballs.

While this tool is one that researches keyword popularity and competition and can be useful for you, the real function of the tool is to understand the cost of targeted advertising campaigns. I'll talk more about this in a little while.

You still need to weigh the income potential using affiliate programs on a particular site. You can do that by analyzing the commission structure of various affiliate programs.

Let's go with our Jamaica Vacations to Go concept. We need to do a bit of research on the travel-related affiliate programs. I'll list a few and analyze their affiliate programs. I believe that your users are going to be more comfortable with a well-known site, rather than a site they've never heard of. An unknown site is fine for cheap goods, like books or toys, but when you're spending thousands of dollars on travel, I think a consumer will be uncomfortable with a less-known service.

For this reason, I will list and talk about the best-known travel sites and their affiliate programs:

- Expedia Affiliate Network (EAN)
- Orbitz Affiliate Program
- Cheap Tickets Affiliate Program (operated by Orbitz)
- Booking.com Affiliate Program
- Priceline Travel Affiliate Program
- Travelocity Affiliate Program
- Hotwire Affiliate Program

Some of these programs are managed through a third-party affiliate aggregator, like Commission Junction or Click Bank.

Anyway, the commission structure is widely different across all of these different programs. Some pay a flat fee for flight books (Expedia pays $3 per booking at this time), others pay a percentage on different services (Expedia pays 2% on hotel rooms).

The providers with the highest commission rates seem to be Priceline and Booking.com. Priceline pays (at the time of this writing) 3% on cruises, 3% on vacation packages and up to 7% on hotel rooms.

From a technology perspective, there are many differences between these programs, but let's set that aside for a little while and focus on how much money we can make (what is the income potential) on our site.

If we use Priceline as our basis for the affiliate program in question, since they pay the best rates, and we focus on vacation packages to Jamaica, we get a range of prices from about $650 to $2,000 for a one-week vacation package to Jamaica from New York. At the rate of 3% that would be an affiliate payment of $19.50 to $60 depending on the package our customer books.

The word "books" makes a big difference here. The commission is only paid when a person books travel. Unfortunately, travel is a very competitive marketplace with many players involved. While the commission is higher than on Amazon Associates, the commitment for the consumer is also higher. The volume of the bookings are likely to be low and the income potential might also be considered low or medium because the customer has an opportunity to shop in many places, including a travel aggregator like Kayak.

Aggregating Affiliate Programs around a Lifestyle

Another choice is to aggregate multiple affiliate programs around a lifestyle. For this example, I'm going to do a bit of research about the "high-rolling gambler" persona. Let's say we want to create an affiliate site centered upon people who are frequent visitors to Las Vegas. We could still use the travel affiliate program to book flights and hotel rooms, but we might want to go more high-end than online travel bookings.

What would a person like this be interested in? What would the profile of this person be? Building a picture of such a person is often called making a "buyer persona" and I'm certain that Vegas casinos do it all the time.

There was an article in the NY Times in 2007 about Vegas casinos catering to "Asian high rollers" – sometimes called "whales" in the casino business. For the purposes of this example, we'll not focus on the "whales" (those willing to bet $50,000 on a single hand or over $1 million over a weekend), but instead focus on the next tier down – the high roller who wants to be a whale.

I go to Lag Vegas once a year and I've seen the type – flashy, rich (or appearing rich) and young. Mainly men. Could be of any race or ethnicity. They drive expensive cars and drink expensive liquor.

What are likely to be their interests? Here's a list that I gleaned from a bit of research about this type of person:

- High-end rental cars or limousines.
- Expensive watches.
- Expensive clothing, including tailored shirts and suits.
- Expensive liquor.
- Tickets to the best shows in Las Vegas.
- Possibly private jets.
- Jewelry and accessories.

- Expensive shoes.

If we focus on creating an affiliate aggregator that brings together the elements that would attract and cater to this individual, we could look into the following affiliates and note the affiliate's commission rates:

Affiliate – Commission Rate (if published)

- Vegas Luxury Rides (exotic cars rental) – 10% commission
- Jet Charter Media (private jet rentals) - $275 on booked itinerary
- Eye Kandee (luxury lingerie) – 12% commission
- Ashford (luxury watches) – 6% commission
- Luxury Link Travel Group (high-end travel) – 4-6% commission
- Leibish & Company (jewelry) - $75 per qualified lead, 7% up to $15,000
- International House of Caviar (caviar) – 5% commission
- Net-a-Porter (luxury fashion brands) – 6% commission
- Kasidie (dating for swingers) – 35% commission

Ok, I'll stop there. I know the last one is a bit sketchy, but I put it on the list to give you an idea of how you can aggregate multiple affiliates even in an area that you didn't know there were affiliate programs.

You can imagine that if you successfully built a "portal" that caters specifically to these individuals and their lifestyle, the income potential is very high across all of these affiliates.

If a person was to purchase goods and services across all of these affiliates and you were to receive an affiliate commission, I have calculated the commission on one person to be over $2,500.

Of course, you don't have to focus on this "high roller" lifestyle. You can choose any lifestyle you like. Some examples are:

- The crafter – scrapbooking, crafts, knitting, etc.
- The gamer – console video games, game titles, gaming PCs, etc.
- The youth baseball player – equipment, instruction, leagues, etc.
- The self-publishing author – tools, books, educational courses, etc.

- The devout Christian – bibles, bible study materials, retreats, prayer guides, etc.

The possibilities are endless. If you are involved in a particular "lifestyle" or are familiar with a particular "buying persona", you might want to start there.

I have a friend who runs a very left-leaning political website, and he makes over $40,000 a year catering to that buying persona.

Creating an Affiliate Website/Blog

Now that we have an idea about our target audience, using one of the methods in the last section, we need to create a website or blog that houses our affiliate links. You can't get automatic recognition of a commission due unless you link back to the affiliate service with an affiliate code. Each affiliate does this slightly differently, but there is a method that similar and common to most affiliate programs.

Registering a Domain Name and Getting Hosting

Registering a domain name has never been easier. I've partnered with several hosting services and domain registration services. On my resource site (howtomakemoneyinyourpjs.com), you can find links to these services (and yes, they are affiliate links – just practicing what I preach).

It was once much more difficult to register a domain name, but now it's easy. You just need to search on the domain name and purchase the name. The cost is typically about $14.00 per year for a non-premium name. Premium names (that are very popular) can cost hundreds of dollars. Of course, your target name needs to be available.

I "self-host" my site. That means that I don't use a service like wordpress.com, blogger.com, blogspot.com or any other such service. I think self-hosting providers more flexibility than using a service. If you use a service, you really don't have to register a domain name.

I will first tell you the story of how I registered my blog's domain (anythingtostopthepain.com) and how you should do things differently. I registered my domain back in 2005. I decided to use domaindiscover.com, which is now owned by TierraNet. I still use them to register domains, but I do not use them to host my domains. I'll get to the reason behind that shortly. I'm not particularly happy with this service or its pricing, but old habits die hard.

OK, so let's say we want to register a domain like "luxurylasvegas.com" to cater to our "high roller" lifestyle customers. We would go to a seller of domain names (and there are many) like TierraNet and type "luxurylasvegas" in the domain finder. If you do this, you'll notice that the .com address is taken. It is owned by a real estate company and redirects to lxlv.com. So, the .com option is out. We can either choose another name, say "superluxurylasvegas" (which is not registered when I wrote this and I'm not going to register it, but perhaps one of my readers will. Just please - no porn or illegal activities. A disclaimer: I am not associated with any website at this address!). Or we could choose the .net option. I am not planning on registering that either – same disclosure for any website located there.

We then choose luxurylasvegas.net and add it to the basket. At the time of this writing, it cost $11.99 a year to register the domain. There is an option at some of the domain name registrars to add "private" registration. It costs about $8.00 a year and, in my opinion it is well worth it. It prevents your registration information from being visibility in a "who is" search. Before I had this in place on my domains, I often got marketing people emailing me (even calling me!) about services they could offer me and my website. Completely annoying.

Once the domain is registered with your information, you'll have the ability to do a few things with this domain. One of the most important parts of managing a domain name is called Domain Name Services or DNS.

DNS is the reason I register my domains with one service and host them elsewhere. It costs a little more to do it this way because most hosting services, including the ones I recommend at my resources site, will offer free domain registration for a domain hosted on their host.

Having external DNS allows me to point my domains at any hosting provider. If I want to change providers for any reason, I can do so without having to move the ownership of the domain name.

Why would I want to do this? I do this because I am free to change hosting companies whenever I want. There is some pain in changing hosting companies – enough that I've only done so twice in the past 15 years.

I used to be hosted at Jumpline, with which I was quite happy for many years. However, their prices kept getting higher and higher and they discontinued the service I was signed up for. They had no migration plan to the new service. I decided to switch to Hostdime, which was far less expensive. Having external DNS made it easier for me to switch, because I could have some overlap time between one hosting company and the other. Once my blog was moved to the new hosting provider, I just pointed the DNS to the new IP address.

As far as some technical details about DNS, the following should apply to your blog. If you are having another person, who is more technical than you, set up your host, feel free to skip this explanation.

There are several types of DNS records. The ones that you need to be concerned with are:

- "A" records – these point a name (like www.somehost.com) to IP addresses (like 66.7.197.4). You should put in an A record with the name of your domain and the IP address of the host.
- "CNAME" records – these are aliases that point a host within your domain to another name. I generally point "www" to the domain name – that is, I have a CNAME record that points www.somehost.com to somehost.com. I do this so that my website will respond to both www.somehost.com and somehost.com without the www.
- MX records – these are mail exchange records. They tell the world which host will respond to email. Usually, the MX record is set to mail.somehost.com.

Setting up a website/blog

Now that I've gotten all of that out of the way, let's talk about what to do now that your domain is up and running.

I use WordPress on my sites. It is easy to work with, flexible and has many third party plugins that will help you with making money with affiliate programs.

You can download the latest (free) version of WordPress at www.wordpress.org. WordPress has some "conventions" that you need to be aware of if you've never used it before. It was originally written as a blogging platform, but now it is more of a full content management system. If you want to create a complex website, I'd suggest that you use Drupal, which is a full content management system with many more options than WordPress has available. That being said, WordPress is usually fine for a small, marketing website and blog.

Some hosting companies will either pre-install WordPress for you or will have an installation program available for WordPress.

The concepts/conventions that you'll need to understand about WordPress are:

- Database – each WordPress site requires a database on the backend. Most often this database is pre-installed by your web hosting company and it is typically MySQL. You'll need a database dedicated to your website/blog. Usually, you'll have to create this database with a username and passwords (for the database itself) before you install WordPress.
- Theme – each WordPress installation requires a theme. WordPress ships with several out-of-the-box. I don't use the themes that WordPress ships with. I like to have more flexibility in my themes. I use either Atahualpa or Montezuma, which are written by an organization called Bytes for All. Both are free, flexible and allow for many options. Some "six figure" bloggers recommend commercial themes (as in not free) for your blog.
- Pages – pages are usually non-blog entries on your website. An example is your About page, which provides information about your, your story and your organization, if any.
- Posts – posts are blog entries.
- Sidebars – sidebars are areas where you can place widgets (see below) that provide additional functionality to your WordPress site. An example is a listing of popular posts, recent comments, categories, or subscription information.
- Comments – comments are reader-supplied content and attached to posts or pages. They allow you to interact with your readers or for your readers in interact with each other.
- Widgets – widget are small applications that can be placed on sidebars to supply additional functionality or information about your blog.

- Menus – menus are links that give your readers access to different pages, posts or external resources. The Main menu is usually displayed as tabs across the top of your site.
- Links – links are links to external resources that you want to promote.
- Header and Footer – the header and footer are just like header and footer areas of a document.
- Tags – tags are keywords associated with a blog post.
- Categories – categories are a way of organizing your posts.
- Archives – archives are date-based organization of your posts.
- Plugins – plugins are important applications that add additional functionality to your website/blog. Plugins are the key to running a successful affiliate site. I will talk about the plugins that have been successful for me.
- Users/Subscribers – users are people who create a user account at your website. Subscribers are those readers who subscribe to either your blog posts or the comments associated with a blog post.
- News Feed – the news feed is a Real Simple Syndication (RSS) publication of your posts. It can be read using a news reader or republished on other sites.

Configuring your WordPress Site for the First Time

When you first install WordPress, you have to go through an installation wizard. It's fairly self-explanatory. It will ask you the language you want your site to be published in. It will then ask you for the name of the database, the user to access the database, the user's password, the hostname and the table prefix.

Once WordPress is installed, it will come with a preset configuration. There will be one example blog post (called "Hello World!"), one example comment and one page (called "Sample Page"). When you login as the "super user" (admin) for the first time you will be placed on a dashboard that gives you access to your WordPress installation. As of this writing, the theme that will be active will be WordPress' Twenty Fifteen theme.

There is an admin menu on the left side of the screen that allows access to the various content on your WordPress site. There is access to the dashboard and to other resources. I'll go through these and let you know what I do to get the site ready for content.

1. Dashboard – the dashboard shows the number of posts, comment and pages you have on your site. It also shows the activity on the site, including the comments that have been posted. On the right side, there is a "Quick Draft" widget to quickly write a blog post. Finally, there's a WordPress News section in which WordPress provides information (usually release information) about WordPress. As you install additional plugins more information will appear on this dashboard.
2. Posts – the posts section allows you to create a new blog post, edit existing blog posts, and create new tags or categories.
3. Media – the media section allows you to view your media library, add new media (pictures, documents and videos) and edit existing media.
4. Pages – the pages section allows you to edit existing pages and create new pages on the site.
5. Comments – the comments section allows you to approve and unapproved comments, to edit or delete comments and to mark comments as SPAM (more about this later).
6. Appearance – the appearance section allows you to choose an active theme, install new themes, configure themes, edit themes, headers and footers, create and edit menus and create and edit widgets for your sidebar(s).
7. Plugins – the plugins section allows you to add and activate plugins. The default installation comes with two plugins Akismet and Hello Dolly. Akismet is an anti-SPAM plugin and will be covered in detail in the next section of this book. Hello Dolly is a test plugin and can be deactivated or removed.
8. Users – the users section allows you to add users, edit users and configure the permissions of each user by role.
9. Tools – the tools section comes with one tool by default. It's called Press This, which allows you to create blog posts from a browser plugin as you browse the web.
10. Settings – the settings section is very important. It allows you to change the structure of your site, to set up reading and writing settings and several other things, described in detail below:
    a. General – In the General section you can add the name of your site, the tagline, the WordPress URL, the Site URL (usually the same as the WordPress URL, see the documentation for detail), the admin email address, the membership permissions, the default role (set to subscriber), the time zone, the date format, what day of the week you want the calendar to start and the site language. You should set these up for your site.

b. Writing – In the Writing section, you can set the formatting (whether to convert emoticons to pictures), the default post category, the default post format, whether you want to post by email and the notification settings.

c. Reading – the Reading section is important. It is the source of many mistakes, including the one I made when I started my blog in 2005. The default setting is to have the front page of your site be your blog posts. This setting is not advised. You should instead follow the instructions in the next section for the front page of your site. You can also set the visibility of the site.

d. Discussion – the Discussion section is all about comments. You can set the comment permissions and some rating information. I will cover this in more detail in the next section.

e. Media – the Media section lets you set thumbnail and other picture sizes. It also allows you to organize the pictures by date. I would recommend that you uncheck "Organize my uploads into month- and year-based folders".

f. Permalinks – the Permalinks section is also very important. The default Permalink structure is by "Day and name". I never use a date-based permalink structure. What I do is use the "Post name" structure. If you write a post entitled "Sample Post" the URL will be www.somesite.com/sample-post. If you keep the default, it will be www.somesite.com/06/08/sample-post (if it was written on June 8th. I find that search engines are friendlier with just the post name.

Step-by-Step to preparing your site

The first thing you should do it go into the Pages section and edit the Same Page and rename it "About" (change the title to About). Remove the text from the sample page and replace it with your "About Page" content. Change the "slug" (which is the URL of the page) to /about.

Next, add a new page called "Home" – this page will be the front page of your site. Add a page called "Blog" which will be the page on which your blog posts will appear.

Go into the Settings -> Reading configuration page. Select "a static page" for "Front Page Displays" and point it to the page entitled Home. Point "Posts Page" to the page entitled Blog.

Go into the posts section and remove the sample post by moving it to the trash. This will get rid of the post and the comment associated with it.

Then go to Appearance -> Themes and install and activate the Atahualpa theme. Once you do that, the appearance of your site will change dramatically.

I like the Atahualpa theme because it is flexible and highly configurable, but the default settings of the Atahualpa theme are ugly! One huge upside of the Atahualpa theme is that the Pages template does not include a "call" to the comments part of WordPress. What this means is that people can't comment on pages, only on your blog posts.

If you do install the Atahualpa theme and activate it, you'll have to do a lot of tweaking to get the site ready for launch. You can tweak this theme in the section called "Atahualpa theme options". While I will not go through step-by-step on how I tweak this theme (it would be way too lengthy), I will note one thing – do NOT use Atahualpa's search engine optimization (SEO) option. There are better plugins for SEO.

You may notice that by default the right and left sidebars are visible and have some default things on them. I like to get rid of these and start fresh. To get rid of the default widgets (and this is counterintuitive), go into the Appearance -> Widgets section. Remove all of the widgets from the left and right sidebars (if there are any) and add a blank "Text" widget to each. You'll use other widgets on these sidebars later. Now both of the sidebars should show as blank. I find the default sidebar templates annoying.

You'll also notice that the Menu at the top of the screen has two Home entries. This situation is because one Home link is created by default and the other is the page we created entitled Home. To get rid of this, go into Appearance -> Menus. Create a menu named "Main". Add the page Home, Blog and About (in that order) to the Menu and select "Menu 1" in theme locations.

Since you do not yet have any blog entries and you deleted the sample blog entry, if you go to the Blog page, you will get a page not found error. Once you create your first blog entry, this error will go away.

Now that we have a framework for an affiliate website/blog, we need to add some plugins that enhance the functionality of WordPress. First, remove the Hello Dolly by going to the Plugins Admin page and clicking Delete under the plugin.

Vital Plugins for WordPress

Some plugins are necessary and vital if you're running WordPress as an affiliate website/blog. These are not affiliate-related (see the next section for that), but they will be very helpful in the operation of your affiliate site.

Akismet – this plugin ships with WordPress. It is an anti-SPAM plugin that prevents SPAM comments from being posted on your site. On my blog, I have received and approved (I manually approve comments) about 1,500 comments. Akismet has protected me from over 270,000 SPAM comments. Really! That's almost 200 times as many SPAM comments as real ones. SPAM comments are a real problem on the web. That's why I never just allow comments unmoderated to go on my site.

Akismet requires that you obtain an API (application programming interface) key from WordPress.com. You have to register with the site to get an API Key. Once you obtain one, you can fully activate Akismet.

Jetpack – Jetpack is another plugin authored by WordPress. It contains a number of subprograms. It is a collection of tools that help in the operation of your website. These are (the ones I utilize on my blog are in bold):

- Photon – serves your images from WordPress' content delivery network for higher performance in delivering images.
- **WordPress.com stats** – keeps track of stats on your website.
- **Protect** – protects against a "brute force" attack of your website.
- Manage – allows you to manage multiple WordPress installations from one central location.
- **Publicize** – taps into social networks like Facebook and Twitter to automatically post your blog posts on those services.
- **Sharing** – adds share buttons for visitors to easily share your posts on Facebook, Twitter and other social networks.
- Related Posts – displays related posts on posts with similar keywords. I use a different plugin for this (see below).

- Monitor – monitors you the uptime of your site and sends notifications if your site goes off-line.
- **Mobile Theme** – optimizes your site for mobile access.
- Beautiful Math – allows you to post equations and mathematical notation.
- Carousel – provides slideshow functionality for your images.
- **Contact form** – provides a SPAM-protected contact form so that visitors can contact you by email.
- **Custom CSS** – provides the ability for you to insert a custom cascading style sheet to change the look-and-feel of your blog beyond the theme options.
- **Custom Content Types** – allows you to create other content types (other than Page and Post).
- **Extra Sidebar Widgets** – provides additional sidebar widgets like Twitter feed and Facebook like widgets.
- Gravatar Hovercards – shows gravatar avatars of your commenters.
- Infinite Scroll – some themes are compatible with Infinite Scroll, some are not. If the theme is compatible, you can scroll down your front page and all the posts will appear one after another.
- **JSON API** – provides information from your blog in a JSON format, which is used by external applications.
- **Jetpack Comments** – allows your visitors to use an external identity (Facebook, Twitter or WordPress ID) when commenting.
- Jetpack single sign on – allows users to use their WordPress ID to login to your site.
- **Likes** – enables visitors to like your posts.
- Markdown – allows you to use regular punctuation to make lists and links without using complicated HTML.
- **Notifications** – notifies you of activity on your site (comments posted, etc.).
- **Omnisearch** – allows you to search through all of your content from a single search box.
- Post by email – allows you to post on your site by email.
- Shortcode embeds – allows you to use shortcodes (keywords surrounded by brackets [ ]) to post content from services like YouTube, Vimeo and others.
- Site Icon – lets you set a favorite icon that is shown next to the URL line on the browser.

- **Site Verification** – provides validation to external sites that you are the site's owner. Helpful tools like Google Site Master Tools.
- **Spelling and Grammar** – checks your posts for spelling and grammar.
- **Subscriptions** – allows visitors to subscribe to comments and posts and receive notifications of updates.
- Tiled Galleries – allows you to display your galleries in a tiled format.
- Video Press – paid service that allows you to embed videos into your site. I use a different plugin for this function.
- **WP.me Shortlinks** – provides a URL shortener that functions like Bitly.
- Widget Visibility – allows you to control which type of page widgets will appear on. Some themes also provide this functionality.
- VaultPress – a paid service that will back up your site.

As you can see Jetpack offers a number of useful tools and functions for your WordPress site.

Google XML Sitemaps – this plugin will render your pages in an XML format for easy indexing by Google. Its intention is to make your site more locatable through search engines like Google.

Head Space 2 – this plugin lets you control the title, description and meta tags of each of your posts and pages. It is valuable for search engine optimization (SEO). There are other plugins for this function, including All-in-one-SEO-pack which many WordPress publishers use. I happen to use Head Space 2 for this function.

Redirection – this plugin will install in the Tools section of your WordPress site. It is valuable for redirecting one URL to another on your site. If you want to change the URL of a particular post, Redirection will automatically enter a redirect from the old URL to the new one.

Maintenance Mode – this plugin will take your WordPress site off-line when you're performing maintenance, like updates to the software, themes or plugins.

Post expirator – this plugin allows you to set a date and time for a post to expire.

WordPress Editorial Calendar – this plugin allows you to schedule posts for a future date and time. It is very valuable if you want to write all at once and then publish over a time period.

Hana Code Insert – this plugin is powerful, but can be dangerous is used improperly. It allows you to create a snippet of code (HTML or PHP) and insert it into several places on your site using a shortcode.

Yet Another Related Posts Plugin – inserts a list of related posts at the end of your posts. In my experience, it is better than the Jetpack version.

YouTube – allows you to easily embed YouTube videos in your posts.

Those are the essentials for operating a WordPress site. Others are valuable in enhancing the site for marketing or affiliate purposes.

WordPress Plugins for Easier Affiliate Marketing

On my blog, I used some other WordPress plugins that aid in affiliate marketing. These are:

Amazon Product in a Post Plugin – this plugin allows you to attach an Amazon product with your Amazon Associates affiliate ID to any post. If you write a book or product review you can have the link to the product directly in the post. You have to make sure to remember to supply your Amazon Associates Affiliate ID and the product's ASIN (Amazon number found in the URL) to the product on Amazon each time you place an Amazon product within a post.

Amazon Showcase – this plugin differs from Amazon Product in a Post Plugin in that it allows you to make a "showcase" of multiple Amazon products that can be placed in a post, on a page or on the sidebar in a widget. The showcase can show all the products or it can cycle through the products. You must make sure you provide your Amazon Associates affiliate ID each time you create a showcase. One note here: this plugin has not been updated in more than two years.

Auto Affiliate Links – this plugin is valuable for replacing keywords in your posts and pages with links to the affiliate product. However, what they're really selling is their $9/month API key that allows full access to their product. The full access product will automatically extract links from several affiliate services including ClickBank, ShareASale, eBay, Walmart and Commission Junction. I really don't like companies that hold the full functionality ransom, but for the purpose of this chapter, this plugin should be mentioned.

Ad Inserter – while I could very well save the mention of this plugin for the next chapter, it deserves mentioning here. Like Hana Code Insert, Ad Inserter allows you to insert HTML or PHP code in arbitrary locations throughout your site. It is great for inserting blocks or widgets that contain affiliate product information.

Calls to Action – this plugin also could be saved for the section on marketing. However, Calls to Action allows you to create mini-marketing blocks that can be placed on your site to entice visitors to join a list, buy a product or download an eBook. The nice thing about Calls to Action is that you can A/B roll a campaign. This means you can create two different Calls to Action blocks and you can alternate them to see which has the best response.

There are many other plugins to create affiliate links. Many of them are just marketing ruses to get you to buy a commercial product. Others are "Trojan horses" that replace the plugin author's affiliate ID with yours. There was a time when Amazon Showcase would randomly replace your affiliate ID with the author's. After much push back and complaints, the author removed that code from the plugin.

With the above plugins to get you started, you should be able to build and operate a successful WordPress affiliate site.

Ongoing Operation of a WordPress Site

There are some ongoing maintenance tasks that you'll need to perform on your WordPress site. You will have to keep your site, the version of WordPress and the plugins, up to date. This is required because of the reality of hacking on the Internet. Hackers are constantly looking for holes in online platforms (like WordPress) and the software authors are updating the software on a continual basis.

WordPress has an automatic version-checking system built-in. The version of the core software, plugins and themes are checked at least once a day to insure your software is current. If an update is required, you will be notified on your dashboard. You can automatically update the core software, the plugins and/or themes from the update area. You should back up your installation (the files and the database) before you update he software. That being said, I don't always make a backup of my blog when I update plugins or themes. If the core software needs updating, I always back up the site fully before I update the core software. It is a best practice to backup before upgrading.

Sometimes an upgrade can introduce a problem on the site. I recently updated the theme of my blog and it "forgot" my sidebar widget configuration.

The more plugins you use on your site, the more computer memory the site requires to operate. A couple of times, when I have upgraded the plugins on my site, the server was not allocated enough memory to run the site properly. I got a "failure to allocate" message on the site. I had to deactivate a few of the plugins and call my hosting provider to allocate more memory to the site.

You will also have to approve comments on the site, unless you use some of the auto-approve features in WordPress. I manually approve each comment on my site. I do this because the subject matter being discussed is fraught with high emotions and there are many hurt people out there who want to make inflammatory comments about my posts. You may not have to approve each comment by hand because of the nature of your subject. I have installed the WordPress mobile app that makes it easier for me to approve comments anywhere I happen to be.

Of course, you can also choose to not have any comments on your site.

It's best to keep your site fresh with new content. I try to write at least five or six posts a week. I can write them all at once and use Editorial Calendar to publish them over time. Fresh content can attract readers to your site and encourage affiliate clicks.

Other Affiliate Site Options

While I just explained how to use WordPress to set up an affiliate marketing site, there are other options. You could use another content management system (CMS), like Drupal or Joomla. Or you could go with a pre-configured affiliate site management tool.

Some software publishers focus on affiliate marketing tools for websites. Avantlink is one. They have multiple tools to enhance an affiliate marketing program, including a WordPress plugin. I am not a member of their program, so I don't have the knowledge to explain or recommend their programs or tools.

Amazon Associates also offers a tool called aStore which allows you to build an affiliate mini-site with their tools. I use aStore to run my recommended reading list.

Another affiliate software publisher is datafeedr which provides a WordPress plugin for feeding products to your site.

Most commercial affiliate software publishers require that you pay a monthly fee for use of their products.

If the idea of building and hosting your own WordPress site is overwhelming to you, I'd suggest you look into one of the affiliate site software publishers.

Conclusion about Affiliate Marketing

You can create a passive income stream with affiliate marketing. Even if it's just books that you're recommending and reselling through Amazon Associates, money is money. Once your site is set up and ready to go, affiliate product marketing can be successful.

The key is to affiliate marketing has been choosing the appropriate niche and providing multiple ways for my readers to access the affiliate products. In my case, I have a definite niche. Even though it's fairly narrow (family members of people with BPD), there are still millions of people in my audience. I've sold thousands of affiliate products over the years.

Since I use multiple plugins/products to present my affiliate products, I tend to sell more as time goes on. Sometimes I use the Amazon Product in a Post Plugin to attach an affiliate product to a post. Other times I use the Amazon Showcase plugin to put together a collection of products. Still other times I use the aStore to categorize and organize a group of recommended products.

The long and the short of it is that you can do it too. And if you do some market research with the goal of affiliate marketing in mind at the beginning, I suspect that you'll more efficiently put together an affiliate marketing revenue stream. I just want you to be aware that affiliate marketing exists, what it is and how I exploited it, albeit poorly. Maybe you can exploit it in a much more competent manner.

Chapter 3: Advertising and Sponsorships

Internet-based advertising has grown exponentially in the past two decades. According to Bloomberg, in 2015, Internet advertising is expected to reach $163 billion. This represents 30% of all advertising spending. By 2019, Internet advertising is expected to pass television advertising in total spending.

While the marketplace for Internet advertising is very big, my experience has been that the income stream from Internet ads has been small. There is potential, but you have to have a lot of traffic on your site for advertising to pay off.

How Internet Advertising Works

Google is the biggest Internet advertising supplier. There are others and I will talk about the big players, but for the purposes of explaining, in a general way, how Internet advertising works, I will use Google as the model.

When you do a Google search, Google provides "sponsored results" at the top of and to the right of the search results. These show Google's advertising system in action. The businesses that are behind those links have bid on and purchased the keywords through a bidding process.

A business will bid on keywords within Google's advertising system (called AdWords). The Google Keyword Planner that we looked at to research the popularity and competition level of the affiliate market space is intended to be used by advertisers to research keywords. In addition to the average monthly searches and the competition level (high/medium/low), Google provides the "suggested bid", which is a dollar figure that Google believes will get the advertiser's ad within the first few sponsored search results. The higher the bid, the higher the placement of a business' ad on Google's results.

For example, if I want to show advertising for my site about vacation packages to Jamaica, I might buy the words "vacations to go" or "Jamaica". Here is the analysis of each of these keywords:

Vacations to go

- Average monthly searches: 368,000
- Competition: Low
- Suggested Bid: $0.87

With these keywords, the average monthly searches are high, the competition is low and the suggested bid is also relatively low. These keywords are probably a good way to advertise your business. If you bid, $0.87, you're likely to have your ad show on the first page of Google's search results when someone types "vacations to go" into the Google search box.

Jamaica

- Average monthly searches: 673,000
- Competition: Low
- Suggested Bid: $1.30

In the case of this keyword, the average monthly searches are almost twice what the "vacations to go" keywords were, the competition is still low, but the suggested bid is higher, at $1.30.

What that suggested bid means is that the advertiser will pay up to the bid for a click on the ad. The level of the bid determines the placement of the ad, but the advertiser doesn't have to pay until someone clicks on the ad. This is called "pay-per-click" (PPC). The advertiser will have to pay Google an amount up to the bid even if the advertiser doesn't "convert" the lead – meaning, the advertiser must pay regardless of whether the lead turns into an actual sale.

There are several other types of advertising fee models. Those include, but are not limited to:

- Cost per impression – the advertiser pays the advertising service each time a user views the ad. The bid is typically much lower than the PPC model. The cost per impression model is typically sold in the traditional cost per thousand impressions (which advertising sellers call CPM).
- Cost per Engagement – cost per engagement is like cost per click except the lead would have engage in some other activity beside

just clicking on the ad (watch a video, go to a certain page, download an eBook, etc.)

- Content (or embedded advertising) – the ad is embedded into an article and the advertiser pays per view of the article. This is more a form of sponsorship, which I will discuss in the next section.

In 2014, Google's revenue was $66 billion dollars. Of that, $59.6 billion came in through advertising fees. If you further break that down, you'll see the opportunity for you to make money on Internet adverting. In Google's online financial statements, they indicate of this $59.6 billion generated by advertising fees, $14.5 billion (24.3% of all ad revenue) came from "Google Network Members' Websites" – and that is how you can make money from Internet advertising.

How you can make Money from Internet Advertising

The section above explained advertising with Google's AdWords from the perspective of the advertiser. Google's product that allows website publishers to generate revenue (the $14.5 billion in 2014) is called AdSense.

AdSense essentially allows you to host ads on your website. If a visitor to your website clicks on one of these ads, the advertiser must pay Google just like if this person clicked the sponsored results from a Google search on Google's site. Google will then pay you, the publisher, a percentage of the ad fee.

In order to use AdSense, you have to sign up for an AdSense ID. This ID will be embedded into the URL so that Google can track the source of the click. Once you sign up for AdSense and you are approved by Google to host AdSense-based ads, you can start making money. Google will analyze your website and catalog keywords in your content to determine which ads will show on your website. Since the visitor is not typing search terms into Google's search box, Google has to determine relevancy based on an analysis of the content of your website.

Here's where the opportunity arises for you. The higher the suggested bid for a particular set of keywords, the higher the payout for you when one of your visitors clicks on the ad. Therefore, from a publisher's perspective, you will want to look for keywords that have high traffic, low competition and a high suggested bid. "Jamaica" has a relatively high suggested bid for a search term with high monthly searches. At $1.30, if the advertiser has to pay the full amount to Google, you would receive about $0.88 for that click (which is 68% of the ad fee and is the current level based on my research). That's a pretty high cost per click.

Of course it is nowhere near the fee that you would receive if you were able to get ads responding to the keywords "vacation packages" on your site. The suggested bid of these keywords is $4.35 and your portion of a click on those ads would be $2.96.

Like affiliate marketing and royalty revenue, I approached Internet advertising hosting with no plan or strategy whatsoever. I bumbled my way through it, without ever thinking about the keywords that were likely to generate clicks and what amount of those clicks would pay me. I was not making much money on Internet advertising before I started to act in a more strategic way.

It's possible to make money with Internet advertising hosting. A case in point (I just took this off the Internet and can't verify if it is true):

One niche marketer reported that he was making $1,400 in ad fees on a niche site focused on security guard training. The site had only 800 – 1,000 visitors a day. That means he was making about $48 per 1,000 visitors to his site. A CPM of $48 is very high.

When I first launched AdSense on my domains, before I wrote my books, I was making a CPM of about $2.50. My sites were receiving about 20,000 visitors a month and my monthly ad revenues were about $50. It's still money, but it wasn't at the level that I would have liked for it to be.

Google doesn't pay out your revenue until the balance on your AdSense account reaches $100. I was not getting a payment every month, only every other month.

How was I going to get that up? The way that I did that was through rich content that took into account the value of the keywords I was using. The best way to increase the value of your advertising is to increase the relevancy of the ads that are shown.

How to Increase the Relevancy of Ads Displayed

Since Google analyzes your content looking for keywords to match to the keywords from their ad database, the best way to get relevant ads to show on your blog is to write keyword-rich content with specific keywords you'd like to target. The more content you have, the better the ad quality should be.

You should also use a search engine optimization (SEO) plugin, like HeadSpace2, to optimize the keywords, title and description of your posts to insure the proper keywords are in place.

Let's take an example from my blog www.anythingtostopthepain.com.

I did some research on the keywords "dialectical behavior therapy" which is a treatment for borderline personality disorder, for substance abuse and for anxiety. My daughter went to a therapist that performed this kind of therapy. If someone is searching on those keywords, then they are very likely to be a good candidate to read my book and blog.

By going to the "keyword ideas" in Google's keyword planning tool, I found that for these keywords the traffic on Google for these keywords has the following profile:

- Average Searches a Month: 27,000
- Competition: Low
- Suggested Bid: $3.50

Not a bad set of criteria for me to target these words to try to serve relevant ads. However, when I went to the "keyword ideas" tab and sorted it by Suggested Bid from highest to lowest, I found some interesting data. The suggested bid for the following terms was very high, even though the competition was either medium or high and the traffic was very low.

- Cognitive behavior therapist: $30.97 (90 searches, Medium competition)
- DBT residential treatment centers: $28.62 (50 searches, High competition)
- DBT treatment centers: $28.54 (50 searches, High competition)

Although the level of searching on Google is very low for these keywords, they pay about 8-9 times the commission when someone clicks on an ad on my website than does the keywords I originally researched.

If we're looking at this from the publisher's point of view, you probably would like for the commission to be as high as possible regardless of the popularity. If one person clicks an ad on my site that was generated using the keywords cognitive behavior therapist, I get paid $21. If 90 people get to my website and all click on the ad, I've just made $1,890.

While it is unlikely that all of the people who search on this term will come to my website, and I certainly don't want to bid on the terms myself (this would defeat the purpose of going after that term at all), if I customize certain pages of my blog to target those search terms, I am likely to get a higher commission.

How does one massage a page to target a particular search term?

To do that you would use the term in several places such as:

- Title
- URL (called a "slug" in WordPress)
- Keywords
- Description
- Excerpt
- Links
- Body and tags, especially at the top of the page
- Backlinks – these are links to your blog from other sites

Basically, this is straightforward SEO, and I discuss that in more detail in the marketing section of this book.

This targeting has two functions and immediate benefits.

1. It makes it more likely that an ad generated from those keywords will appear on your site through AdSense.
2. It will bump your site up in the Google search results (which are called organic site results versus sponsored site results from advertisers)

The one downside of this approach is that the sponsored results will likely appear on Google when the user does the original search. If the link is relevant enough to them, they may click on the sponsored search results on Google before they get to your site at all.

In order to prevent his from happening in this way, you should create content that is attractive to the Google searcher.

Section Targeting

You can also target sections of a post or page for AdSense. This is done by inserting an HTML comment like this:

```
<!-- google_ad_section_start -->
```

And the section is ended like this:

```
<!-- google_ad_section_end -->
```

You can tell Google to ignore a section of your post or page by using the code:

```
<!-- google_ad_section_start(weight=ignore) -->
```

And closing the ignored section with the same section ending tag as above.

Section targeting allows you to target particular keyword-rich sections or sections that contain relevant text to attract high fee keywords.

In WordPress, you can insert these tags by going into the "text" tab on the editor and typing in these tags in the form shown above.

How do you create attractive content?

People are attracted to certain kinds of content on the Internet and within search results. What people are attracted to and what is highly clicked on is this:

1. **Numbers, digits and lists** – starting your title with a number and indicating your blog post is a list attracts visitors. People seem to be fascinated with lists. Some words to use when building headlines are:
   a. Reasons
   b. Ways
   c. Techniques

    d.   Strategies
    e.   Tips
    f.   Tricks
    g.   Secrets
    h.   Methods
    i.   Facts
    j.   Ideas

2. **Explain the article in the headline** – while everyone likes a mystery, Internet users don't have time to open your article and figure out what it's about. You will want to say "How to find the Best Cognitive Behavior Therapist in less than an hour" rather than "CBT and you".

3. **Show you're valuable** – demonstrate the value of your article over others that come up in search results. Say: "9 Hidden Tips for Finding A Cognitive Behavior Therapist!" Your value here is that you can reveal this "hidden tips".

4. **Use Fear** – Unfortunately, fear sells. Some fear/distrust based headlines might be:
   a. 5 Scary Facts Your Cognitive Behavior Therapist Doesn't Want You to Know
   b. Is your Cognitive Behavior Therapist Harming You?
   c. How to Avoid Choosing a Bad Cognitive Behavior Therapist

5. **Educate your reader** – promise special knowledge and skills will be available to your readers once they read your article.
   a. Teach yourself yoga in 15 minutes or less
   b. 8 Strategies for getting rid of houseflies
   c. Build your own computer: A Beginner's Guide

6. **Create Urgency** – Countdowns and time exclusive offers help to create urgency.

7. **Address your audience in the 2nd person** – "5 Ways You can Lose Weight this Summer".

8. **Use Powerful Adjectives** – words like: kill, war, bleeding, fighting attract clicks as do brighter powerful adjectives like: smart, shocking, surprising, huge, powerful, etc.

9. **Use Questions** – "Think you have a good therapist? Take the quiz to find out" or "Ready for summer? Read this guide to know for sure."

10. **Keep headlines under 65 characters** – why? Because Google will truncate those over 65 characters.

Combining powerful headlines with the use of keywords will hopefully attract clicks. You're not going to get a high number of clicks on your ads unless you have traffic.

As far as CPM goes, you can expect the following, depending on your website content:

- General website and blog with no clarified niche: $0 - $3 CPM (that's revenue per 1,000 visitors).
- Specialized niche with powerful blog content: $1 - $12 CPM.
- Product related sites - $10+ CPM.

My blog currently gets about 20 - 25,000 visitors a month. My CPM was around $3. So, I typically made around $70 per month on advertising. But remember that's with no strategy whatsoever. I just put up the ads and got clicks.

Once I followed my own advice (the advice that I'm providing to you now) my CPM has jumped to over $20. It was $29.66 this morning and my average fee-per-click has gone from $0.28 to $2.56.

Massaging pages can be a lot of work, but it can pay off in the long run as evidenced by my increased fee-per-click. I only serve ads on pages/posts that are popular and are set up to serve high-value ads.

You can find out your most popular pages by looking at the statistics either in WordPress Jetpack stats or by using Google Analytics. I actually use both. I only serve ads on my most popular posts.

Sadly, until recently, my most popular posts are about celebrities. I suppose people are fascinated with celebrities. However, recently some of my other content has become more popular than the celebrity posts. These posts have become more popular because other people have linked to them. I will talk more about attracting backlinks and about using social media to promote your content in the marketing section.

The key to successful advertising revenue is attracting visitors and relevant ads. Most people have trained themselves to ignore Internet ads, but if the ads are relevant, visitors will click on them.

The Mechanics of Adding Ads to Your Blog

The first thing you will have to do is sign up for an ad network and be approved by the ad network. Once you are approved, you will be issued a publisher ID and you can start building ads.

On most ad networks you can block ads by category or by domain. This is if you don't want ads from a competitor to appear on the pages of your blog/website.

You can build an ad in a number of different styles and dimensions. The ad network will have templates by dimension (horizontal or vertical banner, square and others) and type (text, picture or video). Once you choose the style and type of the ad, you will get an "ad code". These ad codes are JavaScript snippets that include your publisher ID and the details of the ad style and type.

You can just paste this JavaScript into a text widget to display the ad on the sidebar of your site. You should not paste the ad code into a post or page because WordPress will "format" the code as if it's HTML. This can cause the ad to fail.

There are several other ways to include ads in your WordPress blog instead of just pasting the ad code into your site. Personally, I use the Advertising Manager Plugin, which supports multiple ad networks including AdSense. There are plugins that are dedicated to specific ad networks. Some are more light weight than Advertising Manager, but this plugin is quite flexible. It allows you to direct specific ads to specific pages, categories, tags and a number of other options.

Advertising Manager will allow you to create an ad, put restrictions on the display of the ad and provide a short code to place ads in posts and pages. You just have to paste the ad code into a box when you create the ad and Advertising Manager will do the rest. It also provides a widget that you can place on your sidebar.

The nice thing about Advertising Manager is that it is smart enough to detect the ad network from which you're serving the ad. That's nice because ad networks have different terms of use. You wouldn't want to get "banned" from an advertising network because you weren't aware of the restrictions. Advertising Manager does its best to comply with the different ad network's restrictions.

Advertising Networks

I've been talking about the biggest advertising network, Google's AdSense. Google has spared no expense of making its network the biggest and most feature-rich network. There's no doubt about why: Google makes 90% of its revenue through advertising. However, there are other networks and I will mention the ones that I'm aware of. I have used some of these.

Amazon Contextual Ads

Amazon just recently announced an ad network. It serves ads for Amazon products as well as other company's products and services. The available styles are limited (300 X 250, 160 X 600, 300 X 600 and 728 X 90). There are two nice features that AdSense does not have: 1) you can target a CPM and 2) you can use another network's ad code as a fallback should no ad be relevant in their inventory of ads.

Amazon will also use the visitor's Amazon shopping history to serve ads, rather than using the context like Google does. Amazon Contextual Ads are available through the Amazon Associates service.

Click Bank

I mentioned Click Bank in the section on affiliate marketing. Hey also have a contextual advertising service. I've never used Click Bank, but I've heard stories of people who have generated huge affiliate and advertising commissions.

Commission Junction

I also mentioned Commission Junction in the affiliate section. I have used Commission Junction before. The performance of their ads was not great. However, I used them when I was bumbling around and it was probably my own fault for the poor ad performance.

Microsoft Advertising Exchange

This network is Microsoft's (and Yahoo!) answer to Google. It is tied in with Bing, Microsoft's search engine. I used to use Yahoo's publisher network.

There are plenty of other advertising networks, but these are the big players in contextual ad placement.

Conclusion on Advertising

You can create a passive income stream with advertising on your site. Advertising income is very passive, but it takes skill to get the revenue up to a level that is satisfactory. It takes some front-end work. If you don't do that work, you're likely to see advertising contribute only pennies to your passive revenue stream.

In my experience, advertising has not been a huge contributor to my passive income. However, as I said earlier in the chapter (and I say about all of these subjects), I originally approached advertising in a very haphazard way. It wasn't until I focused on two things that my ad revenue started to make a difference.

The first thing is market (keyword) research. I never bothered to understand how valuable certain keywords were. Once I discovered high ad commission keywords and adjusted my site for those, I started to see some real revenue generation.

The other factor was relevancy. Once the ads started really speaking to my audience, I started getting clicks on these ads and thus started making money. When the ads were not relevant, my click-through rate (CTR) was something like 0.3%. Now that the ads on my site are more relevant to my readers, my CTR has risen to 2.1%.

By combining these two factors, you'll make more money on advertising. High value keywords + higher click-through rate = more revenue.

Chapter 4: Education and Instruction

Many of the passive income experts make their money through education and instruction. They typically offer a free 101 class in the form of a series of videos. The only thing that they "charge" the participant is requiring that he/she sign up for their email list. They in turn use this list to market other paid services, including advanced courses.

An example of this model at work is David Risley, who operates the Blog Marketing Academy and who touts his six figure income from blogging. He offers educational videos and encourages his students to join an "inner circle" (see chapter 7 of this book for more information on membership communities) of members who get specialized access to his private content. I am not a member of his inner circle, but I have watched his blog marketing 101 videos. There's something rather "meta" for me about creating a blog to tout creating a blog for revenue, but that's neither here nor there.

Selling access to educational resources is one way to go if you want to gain revenue through education. In order for this to be successful, you must be able to offer unique and exclusive content.

I'm not selling a "system" although doing so would probably generate more revenue than my current educational efforts provide.

Using Explainer Videos

Another way to make money through education is to produce explainer videos. I have created three as of the time of this writing. They explain various aspects of my books to people not familiar with my work. The way I generate income from these is through YouTube monetization. Basically, my videos have ads included in them, either banner ads or short video ads that my viewers have to endure before they get the content of the videos.

YouTube monetization does not provide me much money. My most popular video, called "4 Rules for you and for a relationship with BPD" has received about 175,000 views on YouTube in its lifetime. For a video that was produced without any strategy, any knowledge of how YouTube works, without any optimization of the keywords in the title or the description of the video, I'm pretty satisfied that it has attracted that much attention. It's controversial in a way, because the community that I deal with is angry, resentful and confused about the subject. Since I present a different view of interacting with someone with the disorder than most other authors, the video has received many harsh comments and many positive ones. As of this writing, the video has 550 comments, 333 subscribers, 807 likes and 65 dislikes.

I didn't intend to monetize the video. I really had no idea it was possible to do so. I was really using it as an introduction to my books. I was hoping that it would serve as a marketing piece and encourage people to buy my books.

Mistakes I made that you can avoid

I made a number of serious mistakes with this video. Firstly, the video consists of a PowerPoint presentation that I give away (in PDF form) at my website. The PDF version has been downloaded from my website over 10,000 times. So, I made several mistakes in the production of the video and its offering as a free downloadable eBook. I just used PowerPoint's timings on the screen. This made some of the slides too short and others too long (far too long). The effect of this is that many of my viewers bail out on the video before the end. The video is 6 minutes and 15 seconds; the viewers watch an average of 3 minutes and 13 seconds. The average viewer also only watches 52% of the video.

I placed the marketing of my book on the last slide, rather than on the first. Because of #1 mistake, many viewers don't even get to the end.

The video is far too long. People don't want to sit through more than 6 minutes of a video unless they are really interested in the subject. One of my other videos is 2 minutes and 29 seconds long. Viewers watch an average of 2 minutes and 14 seconds of that video, which is one second before the end screen. I also made the mistake of placing my book plug on the last screen for that video.

The biggest mistake I made in the production of my popular video was in the selection of the music. When I produced the video, I coupled it with music. The music I used, which many of the viewers disliked, was included in Windows Video Maker. I incorrectly assumed that the music was royalty-free. Big mistake. The music was actually owned by the musician who wrote it.

In fact, this is how I discovered that I could monetize my video. I also (incorrectly) assumed that a video would have to be widely popular for YouTube to run ads on it and spilt the income with me. When I uploaded another video, literally years after I published the first one, I thought to check in the video manager on the stats for my most popular YouTube video.

Much to my surprise, the video was already being monetized! I wasn't getting the revenue; the author of the music I had used was getting the revenue from my viewers! For years, my video was generating revenue for somebody else. You can see how this was a BIG problem.

What I ended up doing is replacing the audio with a piece of royalty-free music from YouTube's library. Once the music was replaced, I was able to start receiving the revenue from the clicks on the ads. I now receive about $25 a month on these ads.

Since Google owns YouTube, the policies of payment are the same as with AdSense – meaning, you have to generate over $100 in revenue before Google pays. That means this revenue is only paid to me every quarter.

This fact leads me to another mistake I made in the use of explainer videos. I use two separate accounts for my AdSense account and for my YouTube account. Do NOT do this! If you do, you will have to wait longer for your money, since each account has to reach $100 for a payout, rather than a single, combined account. I made this mistake all over the place.

The same optimization techniques that I explained in the previous chapter regarding advertising apply to the title and description of your video. My most popular video receives most of its traffic (66%) from the "suggested video" traffic source. This means that viewers have looked at another, similar video on YouTube before viewing my video. YouTube suggested my video to the viewer in the sidebar of the YouTube screen.

Using YouTube Analytics to Drive Traffic

Since this revenue source is essentially an extension of advertising revenue, the same rules apply to the keywords in the title and description of the video. You can use YouTube Analytics (located in the video manager of YouTube's site). One way you can drive much more traffic is to adjust the title and description to move your video up on the list of suggested videos.

When looking at my YouTube stats, I found that the video that drives the most traffic to my video is one called "How BPD forms in a Child" which has 274,000 views. About 6% of my viewers come from the page that hosts this video. However, when I navigate to the page of that video, my video is displayed 16th in the suggested video sidebar.

YouTube uses a method of determining the relevancy of a suggested video based on keyword and common subscribers, likes and other such statistics. By adding the word "child" to my title and description, my video immediately rose three spots on the referrer's page.

If you use YouTube analytics to further tailor your video's traits, including the content of the video, you can attract more traffic and serve more ads, and, hopefully, receive more revenue. My current CPM for the popular video is $11.12. Not as high as my ad CPM on my blog, but it's still pretty good.

There are a number of performance measures that you can use within YouTube analytics to tailor your message, including gender which is shown on the dashboard page. I found that my audience is 61% female. If I tailor a video to a female audience, I should be able to attract more traffic.

I also discovered that 55% of my audience is between the ages of 25-44 and that 60% of the audience lives in the United States. Valuable information for future targeting of current and future videos.

Notes on the Production of Explainer Videos

Unless you have an extroverted personality and want your face out there in an explainer video (which I don't and didn't), I would suggest you use a tool to present your explainer video. The first video I produced I used PowerPoint to make the slides and export the video. Not the best choice in the world.

I now use a service called Powtoons, which provides explainer elements – like writing hands – and other useful tools to enliven the videos. There are many services that provide this functionality, such as Animkaer, GoAnimate and others. If you Google "explainer tools" you can see that there are many. Powtoons has a free service and several paid plans. The service will automatically post the video to YouTube for you, but if you use the free service, you only have access to standard definition and Powtoons will put their logo in the corner of your video as well as tack on an "outro" on the end of your video.

The explainer video services will also supply you with royalty-free music and the ability to record a voice-over for your video. While I don't want to be in the business of creating a lot of videos (it's a lot of work), like writing books, it is a one-time-only situation. I do the work once and it draws YouTube revenue forever.

I have used other tools to do a "screencast" of my presentations. A free one I've used is called Screen-O-Matic. This tool allows me to record a portion of my screen and to record a voice-over in real time. Many explainer videos are made this way.

The most important thing to remember when creating an explainer video is that you should not use licensed music or licensed images. If you do, the artist will be able to monetize your video or file a grievance with YouTube to have it taken down. Songwriters and music publishers are benefiting from people using their songs in YouTube videos without the video producer ever knowing that they are missing an opportunity to do the same.

Use as many channels as possible for your explainer video

Since this revenue stream is coming from advertising within YouTube, it's all about eyeballs. You should post your video in as many places as you can and include it in marketing efforts.

I post mine on my blog. However, I also made the mistake of allowing my blog readers to download the presentation in PDF format for free and without me getting any benefit from the download. What I should have done is either embed the video on a page and marketed it as a free resources or I should have requested that the person sign up for my email list for marketing purposes. I'll talk more about email lists in the marketing section of this book. I made a LOT of mistakes in that department too.

On your blog, you can use the YouTube WordPress plugin to embed the video on a page or post.

Offering Online Courses

Another educational resource you can offer is online courses. They take much more work to produce than an explainer video, but they can be much more lucrative. I plan on releasing an online course later this year (2015).

The online education market is growing rapidly and offers much revenue potential for passive income. If you're an "expert" in the field that you've chosen to make your passive income subject, you should consider producing and offering an online course.

Many of the "make money online" professionals use this method for attracting and up-selling their readers. What they typically do is create a series of explainer videos that cover a set of related subjects.

An example is David Risley's "30 Day Blog Transformation Challenge" which is a free online course that is spread out over 30 days (as the name implies). It is educational and teaches about blog concepts and how to optimize your blog for monetization. I'm not promoting it here; I'm just using it as an example of an online course. All that he requires from you is your email address, which he puts on his email list. Then he automatically emails you one email a day for 30 days to guide you through the challenge.

Frankly, this approach is brilliant in my opinion, because it gets the viewer on the list, engages them for a full month and provides an opportunity to up-sell the viewer. His moneymaking product is the professional system he provides to monetize your blog, the VIP membership (more on that later in this book) and the VIP courses that a non-VIP can purchase and VIPs get for free. I'm not going to attest that he still uses this methodology, but he did at one time.

He can also see who drops out and market to them to get them back and knows that those that complete the online course are qualified leads, since each video is about 5 minutes long and a person will have to commit to 2.5 hours of watching the explainer videos to get through the entire 30 day course.

I don't plan on using this methodology to attract visitors to my blog and to my online courses because of the nature of my readers. Since my readers are generally family members of people with a mental disorder, they don't want to be marketed to in an aggressive way. I have found that there are some others out there in the space I write about that DO market aggressively and questionably to these vulnerable and confused people. I actually care about these people (some are very good friends of mine) and don't want to sour the relationship with an off key note. Of course, it could be argued that this book is an off key note for my regular readers since it is on a totally different subject than I normally write about.

Anyway, back to courses.

An online course should be informative, detailed and contain proprietary information that only you know or have assembled. It should be an extension of your other work. People are not going to pay for the same content that is presented in your books and blog just in course form. It should also be presented as professionally as possible. This is one of the reasons that I haven't already produced my course.

The Mechanics of Online Courses with WordPress

Actually producing an online course within the context of WordPress is not a simple task. WordPress is not a learning management system and is not positioned as such. There are some open-source learning management systems. I tried to use one of them (Moodle) a few years ago and it failed completely. I just wasn't knowledgeable enough about the technology or the concepts to work it out.

You can actually use WordPress to create an online course, but it requires some hard work, some knowledge of programming and can be not for the faint of heart. I will describe how I did it now, but if you want to outsource this function, you can skip to the next section in this book.

There are some services that will host your course for you such as Fedora, Udemy, and Odijoo. I have not used any of these course hosting services. I decided to directly serve my course to my audience.

Another option is going to a studio to produce your online course, but it is very expensive with much up-front cost and much up-front work.

If you decide to go with a course hosting service or with a studio, you also should consider how important owning the customer data and intellectual property is to you. A course hosting service will generally own the customer data, which means the relationship with the customer, is between the course hosting service and the customer, not you and the customer. They will be able to market directly to the customer and you will not. They also may have rights to the intellectual property (i.e. the course content itself), depending on the contractual agreements.

A hosting service will typically provide tools for you to create, sell, and deliver courses. They will charge you either a monthly membership fee or a transaction fee or both.

If you go with a studio, the course quality will be very high. However, like an advertising agency, they will require you to pay a large fee upfront for them to hire actors, write a script, license materials and use their facilities. You'll likely pay hourly for their staff. Additionally, they will most likely end up owning the intellectual property of the work produced. You will, however, maintain the relationship with the customer.

Plugins to turn WordPress into a Learning Platform

First of all, let me just say it wasn't easy. My goal as to create a framework that would allow the following functions:

1. Sign-up
2. Buy the course
3. Get access to the first module of the course
4. Watch videos, download materials and read materials
5. Mark the step/module as completed
6. Get access to the next module
7. And so on.

I had to find an excellent membership plugin to fulfill step one above. I looked at several, including Members, S2Member, Wish List Member and Paid Memberships Pro.

I found that Paid Memberships Pro was the best and most functional of all of these WordPress Plugins. It provides access to payment gateways for the eCommerce portion.

The next thing I had to do was set up a "membership level" within Paid Memberships Pro. I created a membership level that matched my course. That way, each course can have a membership level or you can combine membership levels if you want to bundle courses.

Then I had to set up the cost of the course (really the membership level) and set up a connection to a payment gateway. Paid Memberships Pro provides integrated payment options for a variety of payment gateways including PayPal, 2CO Checkout, Braintree, Stripe, Authorize.net and others. You'll have to create a relationship with one of these. One note about PayPal – Paid Memberships Pro does not communicate well with the traditional PayPal service. They suggest using the Express or Payflow services from PayPal. You MUST have an SSL (secure sockets layer) certificate to collect cash directly on your website via Paid Memberships Pro.

I then had to complete the configuration of Paid Memberships Pro including emails (what do I send someone who buys a course), pages, language settings, and messages.

Next, I had to spend some money. I decided to buy WP Courseware, which is a mini Learning Management System for WordPress. It provides course creation, module support (sub-courses), lessons, completion certificates, quizzes, surveys, and progress monitoring and reporting. At the time of this writing it costs $99 for a two site license.

Then I had to set up a course and the course modules with WP Courseware and associate it with a Paid Membership Pro membership level. I will not go into all the gory details of WP Courseware, which include creating modules, lessons and linking the content together. Finally, I created a course launch page, made sure that only the membership level for the course could get to it and ran a test on purchasing the course.

That's the mechanics of what you have to do to create an online course. And you still have to develop the content. If you're going to be hosting videos within the course, I suggest you use Vimeo to host the videos. Vimeo provides you the ability to make a video private while at the same time allowing you to embed the video on your site. You can specify the pages that the videos can be embedded so that no one else can embed the video.

Pricing Online Courses

Online courses vary in pricing from free to thousands of dollars. Some organizations sell memberships (see chapter 7) that allow the members to gain access to some or all of the courses offered. Universities and colleges have jumped onto the online education bandwagon, putting out "distance learning" courses. Some of these are live, with an instructor lecturing the students and webcasting the course over the Internet. Others are on-demand and are recorded or served as a webinar when the student wants to take the course. Universities and colleges can, of course, charge thousands of dollars for a course if the course is part of a degree program.

I was planning on charging around $30 for my online course. Some of the marketing experts charge hundreds of dollars for sets of courses that teach how to market effectively. I don't think there's any real guide to pricing online courses effectively. I guess it comes down to perceived value.

My course is not vocational, so you can't really make additional money or learn skills to get a better job from it. My course is about emotional skills which you can use to improve your relationship with a mentally disordered loved one. While the course can definitely help my audience improve their lives, it's not going to make them additional income (although it might save them some money by avoiding high therapy bills). For this reason, I feel that the perceived value is lower than one that does add to your income.

Conclusion on Online Education and Learning

Online education and learning can provide you with a passive income stream. Using explainer videos to serve ads on YouTube is one way to make money in the education market. However, the revenue potential is low, just as it is with other forms of advertising revenue. People just don't click on ads very much.

You should treat your explainer videos like you do your blog posts and optimize them for the keywords that you want to have ads served on. However, unlike simple blog advertising, you have to remember that if you're serving your content through YouTube, the interactions with other videos on YouTube can be a big driver of traffic. You need to be mindful of YouTube's suggested videos and analyze how you can get more traffic from those resources as well.

While I went into this earlier in the chapter, I want to reiterate that you should never use other people's intellectual property in an explainer video. This mistake will prevent you from monetizing the videos. It cost me hundreds of dollars when I inadvertently used a licensed song in my video. Don't use licensed audio (particularly music), video or photographs. Artists and publishing companies are on the lookout for this in YouTube content and you'll likely get caught.

Online courses have great upside potential for your passive income. Courses can provide more revenue than even your royalty income or affiliate income. It all depends on the pricing of your online courses and the popularity of the course. Creating online courses is very labor intensive, but remember: you only have to do it once for each course. Once the course is created and tested, the course will provide a revenue stream into the future.

Chapter 5: Branded Products

Branded products or specialty manufacture-on-demand products can provide some passive income. I used to sell t-shirts from one of my sites before I got into the niche that I'm in now. The key to making an attractive and good selling branded product is creativity. If you're funny and unique or if your brand is popular and powerful, you can make money with branded products.

For years, there have been services that allow you to set up manufacture-on-demand products. What this means is that the company manufactures the product when a customer orders it. One of the most popular manufacture-on-demand services is Café Press. They originally started with t-shirts and other clothing items (of which I sold a few), but have expanded to accessories, stationary, mugs, canvass bags, wall art, mobile device cases and other items.

The idea here is that you design a custom item, build the item on the site and sell it. They receive a cut and you receive a royalty payment for the item. Like print-on-demand books, since you're only manufacturing the item one at a time, the base price will be higher for your item than it would be at a retail store. That's where creativity comes in.

Creating a Unique Product

Within Café Press' site, you can create an item, say, a men's t-shirt. As of this writing, the base cost for a men's t-shirt at Café Press is $24.00 for one men's t-shirt (with an additional $9.00 charge if you want to print on the front and the back). It's expensive. That's why your message, brand and/or design have to be attractive to your customer.

If you manufacture in bulk, the price goes down. The base price for more than 72 men's t-shirts is $14.14. However, if you do that, you'll have to order all those t-shirts and take care of the fulfillment yourself. I find it worth the extra money to have Café Press do all the eCommerce, sales tax calculations and shipment, rather than having to do it myself.

An example of a popular Café Press item as of this writing is a girl's t-shirt that reads "I know I play like a girl. Try to keep up." with a soccer ball included in the message. It's a nice message and particularly apropos as the women's world cup of soccer is taking place in Canada this year.

The designer of this t-shirt priced it at $22.00. The base cost for a kid's t-shirt is $18.99 at Café Press. Therefore, the designer of the product gets $4.01 for every t-shirt they sell.

If you can come up with a unique design that can sell well, Café Press will reduce the base price and you can offer a discount on a popular item. The point of all of this is that you must create a unique item if it's going to sell well (or at all) because the base price is rather high, which means your retail price will be high as well.

Some ideas for unique products:

- Humorous sayings (that you own and are not copyrighted)
- Reference to popular characters
- Life Style Products (like gay pride, politics or sports-oriented)
- Funny pictures
- Holiday themed products (like Father's day)
- Saying and aphorisms (that you own and are not copyrighted)
- Quotes (that are subject to fair use)

Deciding on a Product

You can analyze the product categories to select a product to sell. T-shirts generally sell well if you have a creative message. The downside is the base price per unit it very high and the competition is stiff.

The base prices at the time of this writing for different items on Café Press' site are as follows:

- Men's t-shirts: $18.00 - $32.50 depending on style
- Women's t-shirts: $19.99 - $34.50
- Kid's t-shirts: $18.99 - $28.00
- Mugs: $11 - $22.50
- Shower Curtains: $64.50
- Sweatshirts: $37.50 - $54.50
- Flasks: $22.50 - $24.00
- iPhone Cases: $35.00

So, as you can see the base prices on customizable, branded products is quite high.

If your content is themed or your niche is related to a product-type then you can use that to decide on a product to sell. For example, if your niche is about specialized coffee, a coffee mug might make sense. If you niche is about wine or alcohol, a flask might make sense.

I personally don't sell any products through my blog site. I used to with another site before I wrote my books. My current audience is not interested in telling the world they are in the situation in which they find themselves. There's a sense of privacy in the community.

Some other manufacture-on-demand services are: Zazzle, Spreadshirt, Pikistore, Spoonflower and Ponoko. I have not used any of these, but you might find lower base prices at one.

Ponoko is actually a 3-D printing company and it allows you to upload designs for physical products that are manufacture on demand from your design. We will likely see large growth in the 3-D printing area in the next few years, with the cost of 3-D printing tools falling and the open access to design tools. Another example of a 3-D printing company is Shapeway.

Using Drop Shipping to Fulfill Others' Products

While I've called this chapter "Branded Products" there is actually another avenue for creating a passive income with products: drop shipping. I personally have not had much success with this method. I tried it about ten years ago and couldn't get any traction. I suppose the successful drop shippers would laugh at me and tell me that this method has potential; I just didn't work at it properly.

The idea behind drop shipping is that the retailer (you) do not keep the goods in stock or in inventory. Instead, you take an order and have the manufacturer (or large distributor) ship directly to the customer. You make your money on the margin between the price you charge and the cost of goods sold, including the shipping cost.

There are various methods or types of drop shipping. They are:

- Blind shipping – in which a retailer either has the manufacturer ship without a return address or with a private labeled return

91

address. A deal would have to be struck with the manufacturer for private labeling the shipping materials. Essentially, the product looks like it comes from you, but it really comes from the manufacturer or the distributor directly. Amazon offers a service through the Seller Central service that allows you to use Amazon's fulfillment network and get space in their warehouses.

- Small retailers with large items – sometimes small retailers that sell big ticket items will have the manufacturer drop ship the item to the customer. This is especially true on large items, like equipment or building materials.

- Online Auctions – some online auction sites (like eBay and Amazon) allow you to use their fulfillment channels to drop ship items to customers.

- Print on demand publishers/manufacturers – I spoke about this above and in the chapter on royalties. You sell your own books and have the publisher send it directly to your customer. The downside of this is sales taxes must be collected by you if the product is subject to sales tax. Essentially, you can sell your own book for much less than a retailer can, and you place the order with the publisher, using the customer's shipping address instead of your own.

- International drop shippers – in the mid 2000's China-based companies have offered drop shipping services. Some "superstores" that have many products available for you to sell, others offer specialty products.

Like I said, I've not had much success with drop shipping. If you're interested in drop shipping as a way to make extra revenue, I suggest you research it more thoroughly. I just wanted to mention it here as a possible method for making a passive income.

Conclusion on Branded Products

Branded products have the potential to add to your passive revenue stream. The main idea is uniqueness and creativity. The base price point on most manufacture-on-demand manufacturers is high and, in some cases, the perceived value is low. If you can connect with your customers' sensibilities, through humor or brand, the customer will be willing to pay more for the item.

Chapter 6: Donations and Crowd Funding

With the advent of sites like Kickstarter, GoFundMe and Indiegogo, crowd sourcing has become a viable way to raise money for a product or to collect donations for a cause (including the cause of you with GoFundMe). A number of less than intuitive projects and causes have generated thousands of dollars in funding. Some examples are the guy who raised more than $55,000 to make potato salad, the writer who raised over $16,000 to make her go see the Entourage movie (she's donating that to charity) and my friend's daughter who raised almost $90,000 for a deluxe edition of her comic book (the original goal was closer to $9,000).

People DO raise money through crowdsourcing these days. I personally rose over $2,000 for my online course, which means I have to get it completed soon.

Donations

Depending on your niche and audience, donations can be a really lucrative way of gaining revenue. I have a friend who operates a political news site and he raises tens of thousands of dollars annually to fund the site. I also have placed a donation link on my site and I get a few here and there. I also use WP Greet Box to pop up a message about donations when someone visits my blog for the first time.

If your services and products are really helping people, you will likely get some donations. I don't like to ask for donations from my audience and readers because I feel a bit shamed about it, as if I am less that altruistic in my motives for producing my books and educational materials. It's a bit of cyber-begging that I don't like to do. If you don't have any problem with asking other people for money, donations can really work.

The best way to drive donations is to have public-radio style donation drives. You set a goal, say $1,000 and then you count down until you reach the goal. The donation drive can also be limited in time whether or not you reach your goal.

My friend runs these donation drives 3-4 times a year. In order for these to be successful, you must get the donation drive in front of people. The best way to do this is through an email campaign (for older people) or through social media (for younger people who rarely use email). You should probably use both.

Email campaigns require a good list. If you have set up your site properly and thought about the value of an email address, you might already have a solid email list. My friend's site is very member-oriented and membership communities (Chapter 7) are great for facilitating donations.

In building my list (which I'll talk more about in the marketing chapter), I made numerous mistakes, which hurt my ability to raise donations. I have multiple lists and multiple communities and it's something of a mess. I'll talk more about it later in this book, such that you can avoid the mistakes I made putting together a list.

The basic building blocks for getting a lot of donations are exclusivity, value and urgency.

Exclusivity

If your customers feel that they are members of an exclusive club or community, they are likely to give donations. My friend's members are like-minded individuals and are bound together by certain political beliefs. There is a sense of exclusivity from the (wrong in their minds) people who are on different sides of the issue. They feel as if they are within an exclusive club in which the site provides exclusive content to keep them informed about these political causes.

Value

If your work and materials have added value to the person's life, the person is more likely to respond to a call for donations. This approach is the one I take when I ask for donations. My materials (books and website) have helped thousands of people. I get email from many people who have thanked me for writing the books and have made donations to me at my site. When someone's life improves because of your work, the chances rise that they will be willing to donate. I have one reader who gives me $25 every quarter (it's not much, but it's something). When I thank him, he always tells me he supports me like that because my materials have been helpful in his life. I've added value.

Urgency

While donations are nice and people intend to do well by the people who've added value to their lives, many times these people forget. Urgency is important and a call to action to donate NOW. Sometimes it can be the imminent demise of the community – the community is at risk of disappearing for lack of money. The "pledge drive" mentality also works. That is, that the donation drive is time-limited. Matching funds are another way to go. If you can find someone to match the gifts of others, or to provide a bonus if fund raising gets to a certain level, that can work as well.

While the lines are a bit blurred between certain kind of crowdsourcing sites and donations, I know of an arts-related non-profit that raised over a million dollars and got an additional $250,000 from an anonymous donor once they reached one million dollars in donations.

The idea of "for a limited time" works in the donation world too.

Go directly or use a service?

I've chosen to go directly to my readers to ask for donations. I created a "donate now" button through PayPal and the donations go directly into my PayPal account. PayPal takes their cut, which is 2.9% plus $0.30 at the time of this writing.

If you use a service like GoFundMe to accept donations, the service will likely take a larger slice of your donation. GoFundMe charges 7.9% plus $0.30 per transaction. However, GoFundMe will offer you some tools, like the ability to share your campaign easily into social media and could "highlight" your campaign on their site which could generate more donations.

Either way, you have to remember to pay taxes (unless you're exempt) on your donations. I wouldn't want to get anyone in trouble with the government.

Crowdfunding

Sites like Kickstarter, Indiegogo and GoFundMe have proven that crowd funding works. The theory behind crowdfunding is that a creative person has an idea, but really doesn't have the ability to get investors, so he/she goes directly to the Internet to get money in small donations, rather than a small group of angel investors. To be clear, the people providing funding are not "investors" in the business with the idea. Instead, they are given "prizes" based on the level of their funding.

Kickstarter and Indiegogo are "project" sites. If you have a project and you need money, you can start a Kickstarter or Indiegogo campaign to raise money for that particular project. You can't just raise money for yourself and you can't raise money to hire people to develop your idea. It is important that you read the terms and conditions carefully before you start a campaign. Kickstarter, particularly, has some restrictions that you will need to be aware of before you start a campaign.

As a said at the beginning of this chapter, I know several people personally that have run successful Kickstarter campaigns. It is possible. Again, the idea of exclusivity (that only you can do it), value (that the project will add value to the world) and urgency (the campaigns run for a set time frame) are at play here too.

The Kickstarter campaigns that seem to do the best - with the potato salad and Entourage campaigns not representative of successful campaigns - are the ones that end up with physical products (tech products) or works of art (film, comics, video and music). Software projects do much less well.

It is important that your campaign look professional and that you set up attractive prizes. Update your donors often during the process, especially if you're nearing your goal (or surpassing it!).

Make sure you understand the fees, which are typically a transaction fee from the site plus a processing fee. Those come out to 7-9% on most crowdfunding sites. Also make sure If you read the terms and conditions of each site.

Conclusion on Donations and Crowdsourcing

Donations and crowdsourcing can be an excellent way of generating short-term funds. These methods are typically not on-going methods for generating passive income. The level of donations is typically low, unless you have built a strong membership community and have a big email list.

Crowdsourcing is good when you have a specific project that is creative, imaginative and you can convince others that you can actually pull it off.

Chapter 7: Membership Community

Building a paid membership community is the mother lode of passive income. If a customer is willing to pay you on an on-going basis for access to your resources, knowledge and know-how, that payment becomes an annuity and a revenue multiplier. Think about it this way: why sell one book or eBook for $19.95 (making about $4.00 on a physical book) when you can have that same person pay $19.95 a month for access to your resources? Getting a monthly annuity is much more attractive than getting a one-time payment from a person with whom you may never interact.

Membership communities offer you more than an annuity. They offer you the opportunity to market other products and services to your customers. A membership community gives you the chance to actually interact with the customer. You can hear the needs and desires of the customer. You can help the customer first hand and build trust and respect.

My experience with building a membership community has been inconsistent and rudderless. Essentially, I now have two membership communities. The larger of the two has just a shade over 1,000 members. It is my email support list that I operate using Google Groups. The other community is my email subscription list which has close to 700 members. Some of the members are members of both, but the majority of members are only members of one or the other.

Since I had no strategic plan for creating a membership community, these two communities grew up organically. I will briefly recap the story to show you how NOT to build a membership community.

In the summer of 2005, when I discovered that my daughter had emotional regulation issues, I joined an email support list (the largest on the Internet with more than 5,000 members). I began reading other people posts and, after a while, I began posting myself. This list was free to join; you just had to be approved by the moderator of the list.

After a while, because I was participating in both my daughter's therapy and in another physical support group, my ideas and views about the subject started to diverge from the other members of the group. At some point, I developed a relationship with two members of the group who supported my ideas and whose views were similar to mine. I got put on moderation a couple of times for expressing my divergent views. My friends did as well.

In December of 2005, I started a blog to share my ideas with the community. I felt that my ideas and approach was solid, effective and worked well, but the other members of the email support list refused to accept them. I began posting my own thoughts and experiences to my blog. Again, I had no strategy or had I thought through the implications of what a blog might mean or if I could actually make money with a blog.

At some point in May of 2006, one of my friends suggested that I go and start my own email support list. I did. And it began with 3 members – my two friends from the other list and me. I made this email support community free. I approved members based on their answers to a couple of questions when they requested to join. I did this because it mirrored my experience with the first email support community I'd joined.

I had no measured approach. I was doing everything willy-nilly.

Gradually, the community began to grow. I reached 100 members by the spring of 2007. The email support list took quite a bit of my time, because I considered myself an "expert" in my own approach to my loved ones with emotional issues. What I was doing in my family was showing results and I wanted to share those results with others. So, I ended up posting thousands of messages myself to my own list. I would post at least five messages a day and it was more likely I'd post ten.

These messages were long and involved. In effect, I'd created more work for myself with no additional pay – the exact opposite of passive income. I did enjoy the interactions and through these interactions I was building credibility as a subject matter expert. However, one big problem was that I was explaining the same concepts over and over again. I was essentially doing the same work time and time again.

That's when I decided to write a book. It took me about six months to write my first book, *When Hope is Not Enough*. When I published it, first on Lulu and Amazon in physical form, and then on Amazon in the Kindle format, it immediately caused an uptick in members to my support list.

Gradually, over the next seven years, the list grew to over 1,000 people. Many of those people are "lurkers" and don't interact with other members, but some do and through those interactions, some have become my close friends.

I never monetized this community. While I can look to them to donate from time to time, I can't really ask them to start to pay for something that has been free for years. If I could charge each of them $5 per month, I would have a $60,000 revenue stream by doing what I already do anyway. Many would probably leave the list, but even half of that would still provide an excellent passive income. This example is one in which you can see the power and lucrative nature of a membership community.

My other list, which is a MailChimp email list, contains about 700 members. I started this list after I wrote my book and it serves as a promotional tool for my books and "coaching" (which is not passive and I won't really cover that in this book). I send out an email newsletter about once a quarter.

As you can see, I just stumbled into heading a membership community (actually two of them!). And unfortunately for me, both of these membership communities are free. While I can use both as a promotional channel for my books, I haven't yet figured out how to monetize either of them. I mean, of the 1,000+ members of my email support list, the majority of them have already read my book.

What I must do in the next few months and years is figure out how to fit a square peg (2 free communities) into a round hole (1 monetized membership community).

I wrote this book so that you don't end up in the same situation in which I have found myself. You can do it right the first time.

One thing I will NOT do is create a membership community for this book. Why? Because even though there may be an upside to doing so, I don't have enough interest in the subject to spend the many hours required to build an effective community. I'm more interested in my usual subject – which is emotional skills for interacting with highly emotional people. I'd rather spend my time doing that.

If that's the case, you may ask why I wrote this book in the first place. I wrote it to share my experience with you. I wrote it so you don't have to make the same dumb mistakes that I made. I'm a crash test dummy for creating a passive income stream and, while the methods I explain in this book do actually provide me with a passive income, if I'd approached it differently, I'd probably no longer have a day job.

You see, membership communities are a lot of work. Creating new content – whether it is blog posts, reports, white papers, courses or the like – takes time. I just don't want to spend time doing something that doesn't interest me. Perhaps you're the same way. For this reason, I'd suggest, that if you want to use all of the methods in this book to create a passive income, including creating a membership community, you choose your subject carefully. Do something you care about and that you have passion for. I did that, albeit with no plan or strategy.

What I will do for this book is set up a blog/website with links to the resources I mention in this book (howtomakemoneyinyourpjs.com). That will serve two purposes: 1) give you a place to go to find the resources easily and quickly and 2) provide me with a bit of affiliate income should you choose to use the resources from that site.

What I should have done

The whole purpose of this book is to share my experience with passive income and to insure that you avoid all the mistakes I made. What I should have done was start with the mindset of monetizing my work. I was naïve and was doing the right thing for my members, rather than doing the right thing for me and my family.

What I should have done is what I suggest you do: start with a plan to end up with a membership community. Your royalty efforts (writing books), affiliate relationships, educational resources and branded products should all funnel your customers toward your membership community. Don't give away all of your secrets for free, as I did. Instead, create a two-tiered (or multi-tiered) approach. Basically, it's a "premium" or "VIP" model.

Once you have produced work, like a book, don't release it until you've set up a blog/website and integrated a membership model. Make sure that your membership model is integrated with an email campaign manager (I'll discuss this more in the next chapter).

Like donations, successful membership communities are based upon the principles of exclusivity, value and urgency. Your VIP membership level should promise access to additional resources to which the non-paying members don't have access. These resources could be courses, explainer videos, blog posts or eBooks. Tantalize the non-paying members with "sneak peeks" by showing the resource on the VIP membership marketing page with a "VIP only" badge.

The exclusivity factor is important. It's kind of like a country club in which members get access to resources that non-members can only envy. Creating this exclusivity will take time and much effort on your part. It's an on-going task which requires the production of content – which is not a passive activity. If you don't continue to build value in the VIP program, people are going to end up cancelling their subscriptions.

Perceived value will drive the desire for someone to part with their money. In order to create perceived value, you have to provide quality content that helps solve a person's problem. You can make promises (although these should be true) like "I made $100,000 last year with this passive income system and you can too!" You have to deliver on these promises.

As a side note, one passive income stream that I didn't mention in this book is multi-level marketing (MLM). I didn't mention it because I have had little experience with it and my perception of it (which might be flawed) is that only a very small group of people profit from MLM. I don't feel that MLM delivers on its promises.

Perceived value will also drive your pricing. This fact is true in the general economy. People are willing to pay more for a service, brand or product with more perceived value. You will pay more at a steakhouse than at a fast food chain because of the perceived value of the food and of the brand. People will pay millions of dollars for a Picasso, but not for a painting painted by an unknown.

If you become a trusted source of information about your chosen subject like I (arguably) have become, your perceived value will increase. If your methods, advice and know-how have an impact on people's lives, your perceived value will go up and the customer will be more likely to join the VIP program. I've seen this happen in the lives of hundreds of people who are either a member of my email list or have read my book. It's nice to know I've helped them and my perceived value has increased in their eyes.

As I said about donations, there are a number of ways to build urgency. One of the best ways to build urgency is through the concept of time is fleeting. You can do this with promo pricing (time is running out to save 30%). You can also do this with the idea that your customer is wasting time (join today to start making money with your blog). Essentially, it's about you solving their problem quickly and effectively.

Types of Membership Communities

In my experience, there are two types of membership communities. In my day job, I've worked with associations and similar organizations and I feel that this experience confirms my categorization of membership communities. The two types are: 1) Hub-based communities and 2) Peer-to-peer communities.

Hub-based Communities

Hub-based communities have a person or organization in the center of the information flow. This person or organization acts a subject matter expert and produces resources that are distributed to the "spokes" (members).

Information usually flows between members (if it does) through the hub, with the hub acting as moderator, filter and mediator. This type of membership community can also be called "top-down" since most of the information and resources are created by the hub and flow down/outward to the spokes.

If you're acting as the subject matter expert for your membership community, you're operating a hub-based community.

Peer-to-peer Communities

In peer-to-peer communities, each member contributes information and experiences to the community at large. My email support community is a peer-to-peer community in which each member is able and encouraged to respond to other members. While I do act as moderator, I don't tightly control the flow of information between the members.

Most Internet forums/boards are peer-to-peer communities. Members ask questions or present problems to the entire group and other members with experience in that area answer questions.

Some of these communities have a reputation system based on the number of answered (solved) questions or based on the number of responses. Some provide members the ability to vote up or add to the reputation of other members. When the system has a reputation or rating system, the members do not end up on an equal footing as time goes on.

However, this situation is positive, because it helps to provide more visibility to helpful members and weeds out those that are "takers".

My email list community is a hub-based one, with me providing all of the resources. My email support community is a peer-to-peer one, with many of the members contributing.

The Mechanics of a Membership Community

Now I will outline how you can use WordPress to create a membership community. First, like in the educational system, you will need a member plugin. I've found that Paid Memberships Pro is the most effective membership plugin to use. I discussed how to implement Paid Memberships Pro in the educational and learning chapter, and I will not go over that again.

One big mistake I made was not integrating my email marketing list with the membership system. What I should have done is used the MailChimp Sync plugin to synchronize my membership database with my MailChimp list. I highly recommend that you do this if you decide to use MailChimp as your email marketing platform (I'll discuss MailChimp and other email marketing platforms in the next chapter).

I do use the general MailChimp plugin to allow my visitors to join my list, but it is not integrated with my membership system. This non-integration puts me in a very poor position to create an effective membership community. It also doesn't allow me to present a call to action when the person joins the list.

Many "experts" in the field of email marketing suggest that you use a paid service like Aweber because these services have greater functionality and control over the marketing plans and tools than the free version of MailChimp (they have a "pro" version as well).

Another mistake I made was that I offered a direct link for downloading my free eBook (which has been downloaded more than 10,000 times). I didn't require the visitor to provide an email address (at minimum) or join the site as a free member before downloading the free eBook. It was very sloppy work on my part.

You should require the visitor to provide an email address when they download any of your free materials. If I had done this, I'd have an email marketing list with over 10,000 email addresses of people that took action on my site. Essentially, I let over 10,000 qualified leads slip through my figures. Please, don't make this mistake yourself.

What I should have done is required the visitor to create a free membership account on my site and require email market list membership for all free accounts, with an opt-out option after the fact. Then, I should have synchronized my membership database with my email marketing list.

Once you have a person as a member or, at minimum, have their email address, you can begin marketing to them and up-selling your VIP membership program or your courses or other resources. Sure, they could always leave your list, but while you have their information, you should utilize it.

Your privacy statement or terms of use will inform the visitor of what you will and will not do with their email address. Don't misuse anyone's email address. While some people can make money from a paid newsletter, I don't.

There is one individual in my niche who operates a paid email newsletter and I have heard nothing but complaints about this individual. Actually, that's not entirely true; some people have praised him on the Internet only to discover that those people were his paid shills.

Like the educational section, you're going to need a payment processor (like PayPal) and an SSL certificate. You should NEVER store someone's credit card number in your database. Let the payment processor do that. Payment processors are subject to the Payment Card Industry (PCI) standard and have to comply with very strict standards for handling credit card numbers. You do NOT want to be the source of a lost credit card number. That would ruin your community and could lead to lawsuits.

Treat your members with care and make sure they feel that you're providing exclusive, valuable and timely resources. Don't over-market or over-promote.

Years ago when I had first published my book, I had a new member join my email support list. When she posted her first message, it was clear because of the language she was using that she hadn't read my book or blog. After doing this for more than ten years (although it was two then), I can spot a person like that, a newbie, right away.

I responded that she should read my book first as a starting point for her journey. She was initially offended by my "plug" – although I was really just trying to short-cut her knowledge and didn't want to have to repeat to her what I'd already covered in my book. Eventually, after she participated in the group for about a year, she thanked me for changing her life. She is one of my most successful and effective devotees and her life has changed for the better.

I am glad that her story worked out the way it did, but I almost drove her away because of the "plug" I made for my book. You have to be careful not to annoy or drive away your prospects because of aggressive selling.

Conclusion on Membership Communities

Membership communities are the most lucrative opportunity in the passive income game. If you can build a large membership community, you can receive an annuity income from membership dues.

In order to build an attractive membership community, you have to build your reputation with your customers. You also have to provide a sense of exclusivity, provide value and engender a sense of urgency in your members.

It is difficult to build an effective membership community. I have been operating my larger community for almost ten years and I only have 1,000 members. However, I approached the building of that community completely wrong. If I had done it properly, I would have over 10,000 members on my website and on my email marketing list. Some sub-set of this group would be participating in my peer-to-peer community and another sub-set would be part of my VIP (or inner circle) program, providing me with an on-going annuity income.

That said, building a membership community is a lot of work. It requires hours creating valuable, original content and working on your offerings. It's a very time-consuming active. While the membership community fees are passive, operating the community itself is an active set of actions. For this reason, I suggest if you are going to go so far to create a membership community, you do it around something your care about, have passion for and would be willing to make it your full-time job.

Chapter 8: Marketing

Entire books have been written about Internet marketing (hundreds of them) and many software programs and sites have grown up around marketing automation. I am by no means an Internet marketing expert. Rather than provide you with an exhaustive review of Internet marketing techniques, I'll just explain what I do and you can use my experience as a starting point for your marketing plan.

Email Lists

Email marketing lists have been used for a long time on the Internet. My current email list has about 700 subscribers. I use this list to send out a quarterly newsletter with excerpts and links to some of the most popular blog posts on my site.

I review the statistics on visits to my site and try to use the top posts in my newsletters. I also try to focus on lists, since they are big click attracters. I try not to inundate my subscribers with email.

There are some concepts that you will need to know before you start sending email to a list:

List – a list of email addresses grouped together by certain criteria. The general list is all of the email addresses you've collected.

Campaign – this is an email or newsletter sent from you to a list, subset of a list or a set of lists.

Segmentation – selecting a subset of an overall list and grouping emails together by attribute (lives in the U.S.) or by behavior (opened the last email campaign you sent).

Delivery – a successful delivery of an email to a valid email address.

Bounce – an unsuccessful delivery of an email. These can be hard (the user no longer exists in the email server) or soft (their mailbox is full).

Open – an instance of a person opening the email that you sent to them.

Click – the user clicked on a link in your email.

Unsubscribes – the user unsubscribed from your list.

Complaints – the user complained that your email was either SPAM or that they never signed up for the list. If you get too many of these as a percentage basis, you could be marked as a SPAM sender and you will be unable to continue to operate your list.

By focusing on highly read and list-based content, I have been able to achieve many more opens and click-throughs than I had when I first started the newsletter. Like with every other form of passive income generation I tried, I made a lot of mistakes at the beginning.

Just to give you a sense of how this approach has changed my success in email list marketing for my last campaign. I sent my first email campaign in the spring of 2010 to a list that had about 360 subscribers. I achieved the following results with that campaign:

- Opens: 27%
- Clicks: 9.5%
- Bounces: 33
- Unsubscribes: 1
- Complaints: 2

The quality of the list was poor. Getting a 9% bounce rate is bad. I also had two complaints. My click-through rate was low. I have categorized my campaigns in the educational category. The open and click-through rate I achieved with this first campaign was about the average for that category.

I didn't do any analysis of what my readers were interested in for that first campaign. I thought I was giving them what they wanted but there was no way for me to know for sure.

In my most recent campaign, for which I DID do research on my blog stats and on the content my readers actually read, I achieved the following results:

- Opens: 40.1%
- Clicks: 22.6%
- Bounces: 5

- Unsubscribes: 3
- Complaints: 0

When you review these statistics, the improvement is astounding. I achieved a click-through rate that is close to my original open rate. I also was able to get an open rate that was almost twice the category average. I got zero complaints, which is very good and speaks to the list quality.

While I did get 3 unsubscribes versus only 1 from my first campaign, the reason for those unsubscribes in each case was the same: the person was no longer with their emotionally sensitive partner and they were no longer in need of the skills I promote. In other words, they were no longer a customer in my niche.

How did I achieve these improvements?

I did it in three basic ways. First, I looked over the statistics from my blog and selected content that was the most read content over the last year. I also reviewed my Twitter statistics (I'll speak more about social media later in this chapter) and noted the content that achieved the greatest number of retweets. I put the list-based content at the top of my campaign (e.g. 4 ways bipolar is accepted and borderline is not).

Finally, I did an A/B test. An A/B test is a way to understand which of two subject lines attracts the most opens and clicks. I wrote two subject lines for the newsletter. I then used MailChimp to send an equal number of emails to a subset of the overall list. I sent one group an email with one subject line and one group the second subject line.

After 24 hours, the subject line that "won" (the one with the most opens) was used to send to the entire list, minus the test subset groups. In this case, the subject line that had won was not the one I was anticipating would win.

A/B tests can be run in a number of other contexts, other than just email subject lines. I'll discuss A/B testing in other contexts later in this chapter.

Marketing Automation

Much has been said recently regarding Marketing Automation, so much so that I've capitalized the term. Whole companies have been founded on this concept and several have gone public with software offerings to aid marketers in automating their processes. Companies like Hubspot, Act On and Marketo have demonstrated success in the Marketing Automation market space.

However, as a fledgling, beginning concern in the passive income marketing space, I couldn't afford any of these high-end services or products. There are a number of lower cost alternatives to these high-end products. Both MailChimp and Aweber provide Marketing Automation processes. While MailChimp offers some of these processes to free accounts, you will typically have to pay a small monthly fee for access to the most useful Marketing Automation functions.

While a full explanation of Marketing Automation is beyond the scope of this book, I'll give you some examples of basic Marketing Automation functions:

- Introductory Set of Emails – this allows you to set up a set of introductory emails – either introduction text or videos – that help guide new subscribers to your list through the resources you offer.
- Goal-based communications – if a user meets a goal that you set – visiting a certain page on your blog, downloading a free eBook, purchasing a low-cost eBook – the service can send follow up emails based on the goal met. For example, if a person were to download a free eBook, you could follow up with a discounted offer for another eBook or course on your blog.
- Behavior-based communications – if a user were to click-through or donate to your site, you could either thank the person or offer resources that elaborate (related subjects) on the action.
- Date-based communications – if a user joins your list, you can schedule an email for a certain number of days in the future. Or if a person was given a time-frame to accept and offer and did not, you can follow up with a reminder a certain number of days later.

- API responses – many services offer an API (application programming interface) which allows you blog to pass certain attributes about the user to the service. If a person expresses interest in a particular subject, visits a set of pages, takes a course, etc. you can build a "score" for the engagement of that user. Once the score exceeds a certain value, you can communicate with the service to trigger certain communications.

These are just a few of the Marketing Automation workflows you can enable and enact within the context of Marketing Automation. The key is to make your communications more relevant to the user and to drive traffic and sales – to increase customer engagement.

Social Media Marketing

Social Media Marketing is another deep and complex subject. About a decade ago, the title "social marketing specialist" or a similar title did not exist. Entire industries and careers have been built around social media marketing – especially around Facebook, Twitter and LinkedIn.

I am not going to pretend to be a social media expert. Like most of the subjects I discuss in this book, I fumbled into the world of social media, picking up valuable information by trial and error. Recently, WordPress added the capability to automatically post to both Facebook and Twitter. I use the Jetpack plugin to do both each time I post to my blog.

I've had much more success with Twitter than with Facebook. I have little or no experience with LinkedIn, at least in the context of building a passive income. While I do post my blog posts to both Facebook and Twitter, I've found that just reposting my blog posts is not enough to engage my audience and to contribute to my income or my users' engagement.

Of course there are many more social media outlets now: Tumblr, Instagram, and many others. However, I have little experience with them and will focus on Facebook and Twitter.

Facebook

I have created a page for my business-related services on Facebook. The page has the same name as my blog (anything to stop the pain) and has about 250 likes at this time. I don't get much traction from it; although I must admit, I don't put much effort into my Facebook marketing. I do post each of my blog posts to my Facebook page (rather than directly to my Facebook account). That's about all I do. I'll explain the reason in the next section. Suffice it to say that if you want to exploit Facebook for your passive income to the greatest extent possible, I'd encourage you to look for a more narrowly-focused set of materials. I have found that Facebook has been decidedly unproductive for growing my business.

I think it is because the nature of Facebook associations (being friends) has made it more difficult for me to manage my page and attract people to my page. Although I do use the Facebook fan page "widget" on the sidebar of my blog, my page has still not attracted many likes. Perhaps if I put more effort into building a community around my Facebook page, I'd see better results. Yet, like anything I do with limited time, I would rather focus on a less labor-intensive channel – a channel with more immediate impact. I've found that channel in Twitter.

Twitter

Unlike Facebook, Twitter has been wildly successful in building an audience and a "brand" around my expertise. I currently have just fewer than 2,000 Twitter followers. While in the grand scheme of things, two thousand is a fairly small number compared with the millions who follow celebrities and major brands, my meager 2,000 are generally dedicated and loyal group.

They follow me because I am writing about what they want and need to hear. As I said above, I use the JetPack plugin to automatically post my blog entries to my Twitter account. WordPress will post the headline of the blog post, along with a link to my blog post. While that's nice and it keeps my followers up-to-date regarding my activity, it's insufficient for attracting new followers and for effectively marketing my brand.

I started on Twitter in April of 2009. It took me over three years to gain 300 followers. Again, I did everything wrong. I thought (mistakenly) that if I joined, followers would just come. I did little to encourage followers, retweets or favorites.

I decided to use a "feeder" service that automatically posted on Twitter for me on a schedule. Before WordPress released the "promote" module within JetPack (which automatically posted my blog entries on Twitter and Facebook), I joined Social Oomph, which reposted my blog entries to

Twitter. That was a start, but I wasn't generating enough blog entries to draw interest.

Once WordPress released the module that automatically posted my blog entries to Twitter and Facebook, I left Social Oomph and joined another service called Crowdbooster. I found that the free version of Social Oomph didn't provide the statistics about which tweets got retweeted and attracted favorites. The paid version did, but I didn't want to pay for the service.

Crowdbooster did provide excellent statistics regarding my followers' behavior. Unfortunately, after about six months of using Crowdbooster, they discontinued the free service and began charging $9 per month for their basic service. Rather than finding a new service, I bit the bullet and began to pay the $9 per month. Why? Because Crowdbooster was providing vital statistics on the popularity of my tweets.

Beginning late in 2013, I began to do several things that helped my follower count and positive follower behavior. First, I began following people that had similar interests that I did. Twitter sets a limit of 2,000 users you can follow, unless you have more followers yourself. As of today, I have about 1,500 followers. I can only follow 2,000 users.

The key is the users that I follow are quality users and not celebrities. These followers (mostly) have the same general interests that I have.

All-time I have a 21.9% retweets rate (when my followers share my tweets with their followers) and a 13.9% favorites rate (when my followers mark my tweets as a favorite). Yet since January 2014, I have a 25.8% retweet rate and a 31.7% favorite rate (which is remarkable). I have had over 50 million potential impressions (through retweets) on only 1,400 followers and 5,000 tweets. Due to follower growth and tweets span, without retweets, I'd only have about 5 million potential impressions. So, I have ten times more impressions than would naturally come to me without retweets. How was this accomplished?

I followed a path to success on Twitter. I'm not saying that this is the most effective path or the one that you should follow, but this path worked for me. While I don't have millions of followers, I have been able to leverage my followers to gain exposure.

1. I followed numerous people and organizations. I did this in "batches" because Twitter frowns on "mass following". While I could have used a service to research who to follow, I instead used a combination of the Twitter function "who to follow" and researched my followers' followers to find people to follow. I would follow about 50 users each month to build toward 2,000.
2. I started scheduling tweets every day. I tweet around 2-4 tweets a day. These include quotes (which are like lists in headlines) from famous people about the subjects in which I am interested (emotions, shame, compassion, fear), links to my historical blog content (with snappier headlines) and current news stories that are concerned with my interest.
3. I used Crowdbooster's statistics to analyze which of my tweets got favorited and retweeted and queued this content for tweeting again in the future.
4. I responded to those "famous" users when they quoted me or tweeted on a subject like mine.
5. I used Crowdbooster's follow suggestions to follow popular users who followed me.
6. I analyzed my blog statistics to tweet the most popular blog posts.
7. I posted "recommended reading" books for which I received affiliate income.

This method of building a solid follower base has allowed me to gain additional followers and, more importantly, additional traffic to my blog.

Because of Twitter and the above methods, my more relevant content on my blog has eclipsed the "fluffy" content as most popular. For more than 8 years, my most popular blog post was about celebrities with possible emotional disorders. However, Twitter has triggered my more important content – that which relays my message (and thus sells more books) – more effectively. Since the beginning of 2015, my "meatier" content is now the most popular on my blog.

Interestingly enough, with this method of using Twitter, I have been deemed an "expert" on the subject of mental health by the social media rating company Klout.com. All cynicism aside, I do care about the subject and want to contribute positively to the lives of my customers.

Other Social Media

There are certainly other social media outlets of which you can take advantage. Tumblr, Instagram, Google+ and industry-specific social media services are available to leverage your services, content and brand. I don't have much experience with these, so I'll leave it up to you to research other social media services.

Calls to Action

I had no idea when I first started blogging and sending out email for marketing purposes that I needed a call to action to impel my visitors/readers to DO anything. I thought I could just post content and send out newsletters and the customers would come rolling in. Of course, I was wrong about this as well.

In order for you to create a sense of urgency about your offers, it is important to include a call to action in your messaging. You want your potential customers to do something, to take action now. You can encourage this behavior by including a call to action.

I am still rather shy about including a call to action in my content – whether it's an email or a blog post/page. I don't like to look to my potential customers like a shameless marketer. For my general audience, I feel that they need a level of trust in me that would be dashed if I'm too aggressive in marketing.

You, however, don't need to be too shy about including a call to action. Depending on your chosen niche and subject, you can be more or less straightforward about including a call to action.

The WordPress plugin calls to action can help you include a call to action in your blog content. The nice thing about this plugin is that it allows you to A/B roll the call to action, meaning you can include two messages and see which gains more clicks and traction.

Advertising

You can use advertising to promote your products and blog. I personally have not had much "bang for my buck" when I've wadded into the

Internet advertising world. I tried to advertise on Google's AdWords as well as on Facebook with few conversions to sales.

AdWords

AdWords is Google's Internet advertising system that allows you to bid for particular keywords. The keyword research tool I discussed in the advertising chapter (from an ad-serving perspective) also can help you find words to bid on. Essentially, you can research keywords and bid on these words.

When a person types the keywords into Google, your bid will be evaluated and your ad displayed in "sponsored results" above the organic search results or in the right column. You only pay Google the bid price if a person clicks on your ad.

You can set a daily budget, a total budget and a number of other options within AdWords. One of the most important options is whether you want your ads to be displayed within Google's networked sites (like your blog!). If you choose this option, your ads will be displayed on Google searches as well as on networked sites on which the keywords are featured.

Facebook

Facebook also has an advertising system. The ad price and bid are similar to Google's; however, your ads will be shown to Facebook users that have likes in relevant content and interests in your subject matter. While I have not run a Facebook ad in years, you might find that Facebook advertising is effective for you.

Amazon

Amazon has an ad system that I discussed in the previous chapter on advertising. If you're materials are sold through Amazon and you'd like to promote them, perhaps Amazon advertising is a way to promote your products/services.

Since advertising in this sense is about spending money for leads, rather than making money, I'll cut it short. I think that advertising is a hit-and-miss proposition when it comes to a home-based business like I am discussing. Without a reliable subject matter expert, it is difficult for me to recommend Internet advertising as a way to market your products and services. It can be expensive with little upside unless you have a very specific niche.

Guest Blogging

I've had some success with guest blogging on other's blog sites. It is an easy way to promote you as an expert in your niche and to reach a wider audience. While the editors of the sites came to me and I agreed to guest blog, you can probably gain some success asking other bloggers to allow you to guest blog. Perhaps you can trade a guest blog post on your own blog for one on their blog site.

Typically, the opportunity to guest blog will only arise after you've established yourself as a "voice" in the community. My opportunity arose by connecting via Twitter to my followers and the community at large.

While guest blogging is a chance for you to market your products and services, I'd encourage you to focus on content, rather than on marketing. It gives you the chance to establish your voice in the community and to speak from a position of authority. If you discuss significant topics, rather than self-promotion, your reputation will be enhanced.

A word of warning: make sure you vet the blogger and blog on which you guest blog. I have a "competitor" in my niche space (one of the most well-known "experts" in my chosen subject) who decided to guest blog on a site that has since been shuttered by a judge for libelous activity. While my competitor's blog post was I no way libelous, some other content on the site was deemed to be so. This incident was not fatal to the guest blogger's reputation; it was something of a "black eye" once the site was taken down.

Don't be discouraged if the opportunity to guest blog does not arise for some time.

Chapter 9: Putting it all Together

Now that you've reached the last chapter of this book, I want to tell you how to put all of these methods into practice. I resisted starting with a strategy because I wanted you to learn from my experience, as clumsy as it was. As I've noted in this book, I didn't really start out to build a passive income. In fact, I just wanted to help people with what I'd discovered and didn't really think the implications of my actions through.

Choosing the right subject for you

While I have already covered this topic earlier in the book, I am revisiting it now because it is vitally important to your success or failure. Passive income is not completely passive. I spend several hours a day, before my day job starts or late at night stoking the fires. I have to create new content on my blog, respond to my community and interact with my customers. These activities are not a burden to me because I chose my subject out of passion. I would encourage you to do the same.

Although I do make money while I'm asleep, I still have to put in some work in order for the revenue stream to grow. If I had chosen a subject in which I have little interest, this work would be drudgery.

If you decide to implement all of the suggestions in this book, including the membership community, I suspect you'll have to spend more of your time on your subject than even I do on mine. Choose something that you have knowledge about and are interested in. If you do, when/if the "side job" becomes your day job, you'll welcome it. If you don't the new job will be a burden.

Think about what you'd like to spend your off-hours talking about and doing.

Doing Market Research

I did no market research when I started writing and blogging ten years ago. If I had, I might be making ten times what I make now.

Market research is vitally important to maximizing income. Understand your market space better than I did! Know your competition, your income potential and the popularity of the subject you choose.

Use tools like Kindle Spy and Google's keyword tool to maximize your visibility. Choosing the proper Kindle category can improve your sales dramatically. Once I used Kindle Spy to recategorize my books, my sales jumped 25% in one month. You can get access to Kindle Spy on my resource site (howtomakemoneyinyourpjs.com).

Following Through on Your Ideas

As Nike says: Just Do It. Any measure of strategy on your part will be better than my approach. However, you shouldn't be paralyzed by over-strategizing.

I would suggest that after you choose a subject and do market research, write an outline of a book that you want to write. Put the outline aside for a day or two and then start writing. Try to keep on at least a 1,500 words a day schedule. If you stick to that schedule, you'll be able to get through a book in less than a month.

Once the book is complete and the blog site set up, sit back and watch the money roll in. That's what I do!

Finding Resources to Help You

I have set up a website as a companion for this book. Please visit www.howtomakemoneyinyourpjs.com to get access to the resources mentioned in this book.

www.ingramcontent.com/pod-product-compliance
Lightning Source LLC
Chambersburg PA
CBHW022019170526
45157CB00003B/1293